THE CHRISTIAN'S CALLING

The
Christian's Calling

By
Donald R. Heiges

FORTRESS PRESS   PHILADELPHIA

Library of Congress Catalog Card Number 58-11739

Printed in U.S.A.   1-1822

PO4006 I66

FOREWORD

A new interest in vocation is manifest in the churches today. Some of this interest is doubtless related to the great need for qualified personnel in church staff positions. Basically, however, this interest arises from a growing concern that vocation should come alive for all Christians everywhere. If this concern is to be realized, one of the first steps which must be taken is the clarification of the concept. The Knubel-Miller Lectures for 1958 have been prepared as a contribution to this end.

The initial lecture attempts to depict the plight of man without a sense of vocation, especially as evidenced in the world of work and in contemporary literature. Attention is then directed to the biblical view of vocation with particular emphasis upon the calling of Israel in the Old Testament and the calling of the church in the New Testament. The third lecture explores Luther's understanding of vocation, in contrast both to the interpretation of the Roman church on the one side, and of the Reformed churches on the other side. Insights gained from a study of Scripture and of Luther's writings are utilized in describing the calling of Everyman today. Finally, consideration is given to professional service in the church as one expression of Christian vocation.

The author's indebtedness to scores of persons who have written on the subject will be obvious to those familiar with the literature. Many valuable suggestions were also received from the pastors who originally heard the lectures, from colleagues in the field of college and university work, and from friends on the faculties of the Chicago Lutheran Theological Seminary, the

Pacific Lutheran Theological Seminary, and St. Olaf College. To my wife, who read the manuscript with a critical eye, and to Miss Louise Goos, who typed the lectures for publication, I express my deep appreciation.

DONALD R. HEIGES

TABLE OF CONTENTS

1

LIFE WITHOUT VOCATION

Several weeks after it had been announced that this series of lectures would deal with the subject of vocation I received the following letter.

So, you have been chosen to give the Knubel-Miller lectures on the subject of "Christian Vocation." It will be a series that I would like to hear but, believe me, it is not a series I would like to deliver!

Why not? Well, because I have run a cash register at a check-out counter in one of these mammoth food markets from 8:30 A.M. until 9:00 P.M. with an hour out for lunch and a half-hour for supper plus two ten-minute coffee breaks. Each customer wants to have left the store twenty minutes ago, and berates me because the price of food is too high, and has a corn on her left little toe, and three small children who are crying because she didn't buy them gum. The meat manager hovers by to make sure that I, a novice, ring up all the meat on the meat key, because his bonus depends on the percentage of meat sold; and the general manager is tearing his hair because the district manager is due any minute, and the lines are too long, and last week was a bad week, etc. And I must continue to smile at and greet *every* customer. By the way, did you plan to speak on the "joy" of work?

I have also weighed and banded bananas for six solid hours. Frankly, it isn't very "creative." Did I band the bananas "to the glory of God"? No, I did not! I just banded them because I had to. When I weighed cabbages I tried to be honest, and there is a bit of inner reward to that, I guess; but then I thought about the produce manager and his sick wife and small children and the narrow margin of his profit—one cent per dollar of sales.

Just where is "vocation" for the vast majority of people in jobs like this? Where is it when the coffee break is the peak experience of the day? Where is it when you work simply because you get paid on Friday, and you've got to do *something* because that's the way things are?

When I read this letter to my family one evening my high school daughter exclaimed: "And you're going to try to answer that! It can't be done. Vocation will not stretch that far."

She may be right. It may be that the concept of vocation cannot be stretched to cover the check-out girls in hundreds of supermarkets across the land. And what about the millions and millions of other human beings in America, and throughout the whole world, who toil at tasks that are uncreative, monotonous, and deadening? What has the church to say to them? Is the Christian view of vocation relevant to their situations?

These and many similar questions lay back of these lectures. No attempt will be made to answer all of them; in fact, only a few of the questions, the most basic, can even be raised. It is a vast field, and the literature is as extensive as is the confusion on the subject. Coupled with this confusion is a widespread feeling of uneasiness: What has happened to vocation, anyhow? Has something dropped out along the way? If so, what is it?

And then there is the critical shortage of persons for the so-called "church vocations": the ordained ministry, missions, the diaconate, parish work, Christian education. The concern of church officials over this shortage of qualified personnel is almost reaching the panic stage. All sorts of high-pressure methods are being used to produce "more men for the ministry," and for related fields of service. At times it is difficult to distinguish between the recruitment techniques of industry and those being employed by the churches.

Many reasons have been advanced to account for this shortage, such as: The normal annual increase in the number of persons available has not been enough to meet the personnel needs of churches which are growing and expanding at an extraordinary rate; The inducements to enter other fields of work are today unusually appealing; Church employment has become so secularized that it no longer challenges the sensitive and deeply committed Christian; etc. Seldom if ever does it occur to anyone that the shortage of persons for "church vocations" may reflect the disappearance of a dynamic and valid concept of vocation per se, that is, as applicable to the lives of all Christians.

The purpose of these lectures is to explore the meaning of vocation and the difference vocation can make in the life of a Christian. Not until we reach the fourth lecture will an attempt be made to describe a concept of vocation relevant to the contemporary scene. To do so prior to an examination of vocation in the Bible and in the writings of Martin Luther would be illogical and irresponsible. Nevertheless, in order to depict "Life Without Vocation" it is necessary to indicate, at least in an elementary way, what is meant by vocation. This can be done in two simple affirmations: (a) Vocation takes within its sweep the totality of a person's life—not just remunerative employment. (b) Vocation is life lived within the purpose and power of God. At this point we are interested in seeing what happens when life is not lived within his purpose and power. Specifically, we shall first take a look at work without meaning, and then push back the horizons and gaze upon life without meaning.

What's the point of working?

Let us return to the letter quoted at the beginning of this lecture and to the basic question it raises: "Just where is vocation for the vast majority in jobs like this?" Although vocation is much more inclusive than work, it does include work, and the question is quite properly asked.

Long, long ago—thousands of years before supermarkets and assembly lines—the author of Ecclesiastes raised a similar question. "What has a man from all the toil and strain with which he toils beneath the sun? For all his days are full of pain, and his work is a vexation; even in the night his mind does not rest" (2:22-23). Indeed, ever since his expulsion from Eden man has known the vexation of toil, but in many areas of contemporary life that vexation has become destructive of the human spirit.

The issue here is not basically one of drudgery. Work can make terrible demands on the body or the mind; it can be dirty, disagreeable, dangerous, deadening, and deafening, and still not be inherently destructive of the human spirit. This is not to say that dirt, disagreeableness, danger, monotony, and noise should not be reduced to a minimum. In this regard we have come a long way since the early days of Western industrialism when women and children as well as men were subjected to bestial treatment in the factories and mines. But the most serious curse which can befall labor is meaninglessness. Drudgery can be borne within the context of meaning, but when man sees no point, no meaning, no significance in his toil, then the soul is endangered, and the only healthy reaction is one of abandoning the job.

Many years ago I heard a story about a gang of laborers digging holes in a street. After they had blasted through six inches of asphalt and concrete with a compressed air hammer, and had shoveled out rock, sand, and soil to a depth of about five feet, the boss inspected the hole and yelled, "Okay, fill her up." Then they would move down the street some distance, proceed to dig another hole, and when it was five feet deep the boss would look at it and yell, "Okay, fill her up." And so it went on all morning. After lunch the men gathered around the boss and announced: "We quit. Pay us off." The astounded foreman asked if the work was too hard or the pay too low, but the men just shook their heads. Finally, one of them blurted out: "We quit because no one is going to make damn fools of us. Just diggin' holes and fillin' 'em up again!" "Oh," said the boss, "is that it? Well, you see, the records for this old section of the

city have been lost, and we're trying to find the water mains."
The men went back to work. Deep down a human being wants
to see some point to what he is doing, even if what he is doing
makes no great demands upon the mind or body.

Robert Michaelsen emphasizes this facet of human nature in
his criticism of the classic concept of "the economic man" in
industrial development.

It appears that although much of the approach to the worker—
both by industrialists and union leaders—has been guided by the
"myth" of "economic man," still the over-all reaction of the worker
has demonstrated his basic recognized and unrecognized interest in
far more than material reward. He seeks much more out of work
than his pay check. He wants some sense of his role in the total
enterprise—a feeling that his work means something in itself, and
that there is a future in it beyond the tangible financial return. He
longs for a place in the industrial community—some satisfaction of
his urge as a social individual. Possibly he would also like a fuller
voice in the decision-making that takes place in the industrial community, and some sense of responsibility for the condition and use
of industrial production. Studies of industrial workers . . . seem to
indicate that when the worker feels that he is getting some of these
things, he finds meaning and joy in his work almost regardless of
economic incentive.[1]

And this is where vocation comes into the picture, because
vocation gives meaning, significance to all of life, including labor.
Obviously there are many possible levels of meaning; vocation is
the level of meaning created by the initiative and action of God
himself. When vocation disappears from life, sufficient meaning
to keep a man going is sometimes found on lower levels—in
certain eras, under certain conditions, or in certain occupations.
For example, a physician who is an avowed atheist may gain
sufficient technical satisfaction from his work to keep him at it

---

[1] John Oliver Nelson (ed.), *Work and Vocation* (New York: Harper,
1954), p. 142.

with enduring interest. A case in point is Dr. Lucas Marsh in the novel *Not As a Stranger*, by Morton Thompson.[2]

The tragedy is that the methods of mass production in modern industry do not by and large provide those "certain conditions" necessary to establish meaning on a level lower than that of vocation, and since millions employed in industry have no sense of vocation, toil in itself is devoid of significance. Another story, which is making the rounds in several versions, will make this fact unforgettable.

Three Europeans on a tour of industry in the United States were visiting a mammoth manufacturing plant, and stopped to chat with a man operating a machine which turned out a slightly curved piece of metal about five inches long. Here is how the conversation went.

QUESTION: "How long have you been working at this machine?"

ANSWER: "Six years."

QUESTION: "Just what are you making?"

ANSWER: "U273."

QUESTION: "Yes, but what is the name of it?"

ANSWER: "Name? It has no name—just U273."

QUESTION: "Well, then, what is U273 for—what purpose does it serve?"

ANSWER: "What's it for? How should I know?"

QUESTION: "Why do you keep on making U273?"

ANSWER: "It pays $1.90 an hour. Hey, are you guys some of them there communists?"

End of conversation. Mass production meaningless? Ah yes, so meaningless, and so taken for granted, that if one pushes the question "why?" too far he is liable to be suspected of being subversive!

That much mass production reduces human beings to the status of almost unconscious cogs in machines is no longer dis-

[2] New York: Scribner's, 1954.

puted. In fact, constant repetition has rendered the charge hackneyed. But its implications must be faced. A man who is condemned to operate a machine, which he does not own, to produce an object labeled U273 to be incorporated into a product which he did not design and which he may never see except in advertisements, for a company to which he does not belong and over which he has no control and from which he may receive his layoff slip at any time—such a man, finding no meaning in his work, either finds some significance to his life elsewhere—in a hobby, commercialized entertainment, his family—or he sinks more and more deeply into the quicksand of despair.

Industrialists, of course, have not been unaware of this problem. In the words of the Chairman of General Foods Corporation: "You can buy a man's time, you can buy a man's physical presence at a given place; you can even buy a measured number of skilled muscular motions per hour or day. But you cannot buy enthusiasm; you cannot buy loyalty; you cannot buy devotion of hearts, minds, and souls." [3] And so industrialists have called in public relations and personnel management experts to solve the problem. As a result all sorts of gimmicks have been introduced—music piped into factories, intramural sports, counseling services, profit-sharing schemes, etc.—and these have doubtless helped to make the workers less restive with their lot, but it cannot be said that they have solved the basic problem. Furthermore, one gets the impression that these clever personnel management methods are being used to manipulate people rather than being introduced out of a genuine concern for their welfare. In fact, the corporation executive quoted above bluntly states that "the human will to work" is "the most promising single source of *productivity* [sic!]."

The void which exists in the absence of vocation on the machine level extends also into the higher echelons of the

[3] *Time*, April 14, 1952, p. 97.

industrial order. "The machine man" of the factories has his counterpart in "the organization man" of the administrative offices, as so strikingly and terrifyingly depicted by William H. Whyte.[4] The latter is chained to the organization just as surely as the former is chained to the machine, except that the man in the factory seldom if ever worships the machine in contrast to the man in the administrative offices who tends to deify the organization. In either case the integrity and initiative of the individual have almost disappeared.

Depersonalization proceeds apace because, on the one hand, only the machine matters and, on the other hand, only the organization matters. And yet there seems to be this difference: men in the factory are forced to become robots in order to survive, while men in the administrative offices are willing to lose themselves in the organization because they believe this is the right way to get the enormous tasks in the nation done and to realize the primary objectives of their own lives. As Whyte points out,[5] the members of the managerial class seek meaning through community, but commit the fallacy of regarding the organization as community when actually it is merely a form of collectivism.

Reference has just been made to "the primary objectives of their own lives," i.e., those of the junior or senior executives. The list is well known: occupational and financial security, recognition in a particular field of competence, family stability and comfort, social status and perhaps prestige, leisure enough to enjoy "the good things of life," and early retirement in order to continue to enjoy these good things of life on a full-time basis just as long as possible. In his study of *Changing Values in College*,[6] Philip E. Jacob discovered that these life objectives are rather well formulated during the undergraduate years and are

---

[4] *The Organization Man* (New York: Doubleday, 1957).
[5] *Ibid.*, chaps. IV and V.
[6] New York: Harper, 1957.

the common property of the vast majority of the nation's college and university students. *Time* magazine in a survey of the attitudes of "the younger generation" included an anecdote which, although it has been widely quoted, bears quoting again.

On a sunny Sunday not long ago, Sociology Professor Carr B. Lavell of George Washington University took one of his students on a fishing trip. He is a brilliant student, president of his class, a big man on campus, evidently with a bright future in his chosen field, medicine. In the bracing air, professor and student had a quiet talk. Why had he gone into medicine, asked the professor. Answer: medicine looked lucrative. What did he want to do as a doctor? Get into the speciality that offered the biggest fees. Did he think that a doctor owed some special service to the community? Probably not. "I am just like any one else," said the student. "I just want to prepare myself so that I can get the most out of it for me. I hope to make a lot of money in a hurry. I'd like to retire in about ten years and do the things I really want." And what are those? "Oh," said the brilliant student, "fishing, traveling, taking it easy." [7]

The article proceeds to report that such an orientation to life is typical not only of the great majority of medical students but also of those going into the other so-called "professions."

In short, what those in the managerial class of industry want out of life is indistinguishable from what those in the professions seek. A difference is that the former seek these objectives through participation in a managerial collective whereas the latter seek them primarily on an individualistic basis, although with reference to the field of medicine, for example, the power of collective action through the A.M.A., the local medical associations, and hospital staffs cannot be overlooked. The fact remains that in both categories the chief ends of life are projected in self-centered and materialistic terms.

This is a glimpse of work today without vocation. I say "a glimpse" advisedly because no attempt has been made to survey

[7] *Time*, November 5, 1951.

the entire occupational field. What has been seen, however, in factory workers, in the managers of industry, and in the professions is indicative of the orientation of almost all work in our culture. Vocation, except as a casual synonym for occupation, has been exiled from the world of toil.

Attention has been focused on that segment of life known as "work" partly because it is such a large segment of man's life and partly because those who still refer occasionally to vocation restrict its applicability to work. Since it is a thesis of these lectures that vocation encompasses the whole of human existence, it now becomes necessary to take a look at life without vocation.

What's the point of living?

When a human being begins to wrestle with the question, "Why work?" he is usually not too far removed from a much more devastating question, namely, "Why live?" John Oliver Nelson observes[8] that if a worker went to a typical personnel department of a corporation with the query, "Why work at all? Why human existence, and human relations? Why live?" he would probably be referred to a psychiatrist, because it would appear that the man is dangerously close to going off the deep end. And indeed he is close to the deep end—the deep end of meaninglessness!

Of course, this problem is not unique to our times. Individuals have doubtless struggled with it since the dawn of self-consciousness. The author of Ecclesiastes, who has already been quoted, is one of these individuals. He writes:

I have seen everything that is done under the sun; and behold, all is vanity and a striving after wind. What is crooked cannot be made straight, and what is lacking cannot be numbered. . . . For of the wise man as of the fool there is no enduring remembrance, seeing that in the days to come all will have been long forgotten. How the wise

[8] *Op. cit.*, p. 22.

man dies just like a fool! So I hated life, because what is done under the sun was grievous to me; for all is vanity, and a striving after wind. . . . And I turned about and gave my heart up to despair . . . (1:14-15; 2:16-18, 20).

Yes, in every generation there have been individuals overwhelmed with the sense of futility. But periodically in the course of human history whole cultures seem to become afflicted with the virus of meaninglessness. And this seems to be true today of the culture of the West. Obviously the disease is not as advanced in some sections of Western culture as in others, but anyone with a modicum of intelligence can detect evidences of the virus almost everywhere.

Many of our poets, novelists, dramatists, philosophers, and theologians have been preoccupied for more than a quarter of a century with the anatomy of meaninglessness. A few "samples" of this literature will provide a background for consideration of the problem at hand. These samplings can best be understood as footnotes to the morphology of despair, succinctly stated by the late Joseph Fort Newton in these words: "When a man loses faith in God, he worships humanity; when faith in humanity fails, he worships science, as so many are trying to do today. When faith in science fails, man worships himself, and at the altar of his own idolatry he receives a benediction of vanity. Hence the tedious egotism of our day, when men are self-centered and self-obsessed, unable to get themselves out of their own hands." [9]

T. S. Eliot was among the first of twentieth-century English writers to depict modern man stripped of meaning. His poem *The Waste Land* has been cited by almost every diagnostician of our cultural malaise—and deservedly. The aimlessness, the emptiness, the aridness of life has seldom been so powerfully portrayed.

[9] The locus of this quotation cannot be identified.

Here is no water but only rock
Rock and no water and the sandy road
The road winding above among the mountains
Which are mountains of rock without water
If there were water we should stop and drink
Amongst the rock one cannot stop or think
Sweat is dry and feet are in the sand
If only there were water amongst the rock
Dead mountain mouth of carious teeth that cannot spit
Here one can neither stand nor lie nor sit
There is not even silence in the mountains
But dry sterile thunder without rain
There is not even solitude in the mountains
But red sullen faces sneer and snarl
From doors of mud cracked houses
                              If there were water
And no rock
If there were rock
And also water
And water
A spring
A pool among the rock
If there were the sound of water only
Not the cicada
And dry grass singing
But the sound of water over a rock
Where the hermit-thrush sings in the pine trees
Drip drop drip drop drop drop drop
But there is no water[10]

The imagery is so biblical through and through that scores of passages, especially from the prophets, come to mind, as, for example this from Jeremiah (2:12-13): "Be appalled, O heavens, at this, be shocked, be utterly desolate, says the Lord, for my people have committed two evils: they have forsaken me, the fountain of living waters, and hewed out cisterns for themselves, broken cisterns, that can hold no water."

[10] *Complete Poems and Plays, 1909-1950* (New York: Harcourt, Brace, 1952), pp. 47-48.

Symbolism is replaced by conceptualization in the first chorus from Eliot's "The Rock," but the mood is similar to that of *The Waste Land*—an aching sense of something missing, the one thing needful.

> The endless cycle of idea and action,
> Endless invention, endless experiment,
> Brings knowledge of motion, but not of stillness;
> Knowledge of speech, but not of silence;
> Knowledge of words, and ignorance of the Word.
> All our knowledge brings us nearer to our ignorance,
> All our ignorance brings us nearer to death,
> But nearness to death no nearer to God.
> Where is the Life we have lost in living?
> Where is the wisdom we have lost in knowledge?
> Where is the knowledge we lost in information? [11]

Knowledge of words, and ignorance of the Word—this is the plight of contemporary man in his wasteland.

In our disrupted world we well know what "displaced persons" are—those people driven or self-exiled from their homelands who wander over the face of the earth. Today this is the spiritual state of millions of men and women—displaced persons, homeless in the cosmos and homeless among their own kind, with nowhere to lay their heads, nowhere to rest their souls. Spokesman for the displaced souls is Franz Kafka, who has been described as "the most representative figure in twentieth-century literature." In fact, W. H. Auden goes so far as to say: "Had one to name the artist who comes nearest to bearing the same kind of relation to our age that Dante, Shakespeare, and Goethe bore to theirs, Kafka is the first we would think of." [12] He is the writer par excellence of alienation.

To a greater or lesser degree, creative literature is always

[11] *Ibid.*, p. 97.
[12] Nathan A. Scott, Jr. (ed.), *The Tragic Vision and the Christian Faith* (New York: Association Pr., 1957), pp. 281-82.

autobiographical, but this was especially true of Kafka. In laying his own soul bare he laid bare the souls of his contemporaries. "I have been forty years wandering from Canaan. . . . It is indeed a kind of wandering in the wilderness in reverse that I am undergoing." [13] As J. Hillis Miller points out, for Kafka "the entire human community is in the desert, attempting to build an impious tower of Babel to scale heaven, but really cutting itself off more and more from God and creating a self-enclosed structure of purely human values and institutions. . . . Once, long ago, as Kafka says in one of his very last stories, the Word was close to man, and interpenetrated his world, but now it has withdrawn altogether, and all mankind is lost." [14] The imagery of the desert reminds one of Eliot's *The Waste Land*. Kafka describes his own condition (and, therefore, the condition of every man) in terms of dryness, of being deprived of water. He finds the "well gone dry, water at an unattainable depth and no certainty it is there." [15]

One of the most horrible stories written by Kafka is "The Metamorphosis." [16] Gregor Samsa, an undistinguished traveling salesman, becomes so alienated from his community and his family that he wakes up one morning to discover that he has been transformed into an enormous cockroach. This amazing event makes his alienation complete. His "human" consciousness remains, but the ability to communicate with his family is completely gone. Physically he shares the same house (locked in his own room or released now and then to look at the family scene), but he could just as well have been a million miles away from his father and mother and sister because there is no way to let them know his thoughts. In his excruciating agony the only escape is death but, unlike Willie Loman in J. Arthur Miller's

[13] Quoted by J. Hillis Miller, Jr., in Scott (ed.), *The Tragic Vision and the Christian Faith*, p. 282.

[14] *Ibid.*, p. 285.

[15] *Ibid.*, p. 291.

[16] *Selected Short Stories* (New York: Modern Library, 1952), pp. 19-89.

play, *The Death of a Salesman*,[17] he cannot destroy himself. His fate is to die slowly until at the last little more remains but the dry shell and emptiness within.

But man's alienation is basically vertical, not merely horizontal. Kafka calls attention not only to man's isolation from his fellows, but also to his isolation from the ground of his being. In other words, his haunting concern was the God-relationship which he knew only negatively as something necessary but not realizable. "There is a goal, but no way; what we call the way is only wavering." [18] In his despair and frustration he charges that original sin, supposedly committed by man against God, was actually "committed upon him " [19]

According to Kafka, deep down in the memory of each man cast adrift on the void of the contemporary world is a picture of human existence characterized by ordered relationships, by a structure in which he once had a niche to fill. The fleeting perception of such a picture merely deepens his nostalgia, his alienation, his frustration; it does not give him a cue to the resolution of his predicament. Here is Kafka's description of life without vocation as sensed by modern man.

He was once part of a monumental group. Round some elevated figure or other in the center were ranged in carefully thought-out order symbolical images of the military caste, the arts, the sciences, the handicrafts. He was one of those many figures. Now the group is long since dispersed, or at least he has left it and makes his way through life alone. He no longer has even his old vocation; indeed he has actually forgotten what he once represented. Probably it is the very forgetting that gives rise to a certain melancholy, uncertainty, unrest, a certain longing for vanished ages, darkening the present.[20]

[17] New York: Viking Pr., 1949.
[18] Franz Kafka, *The Great Wall of China* (London: Secker, 1933), p. 259.
[19] *Ibid.*, p. 246.
[20] *Ibid.*, pp. 244-45.

Then there is Jean-Paul Sartre, who cannot be passed by in any consideration of the blight of futility. Whatever else may be said about this controversial figure, it must be affirmed that he is the master at depicting human beings who are trapped, not as men are trapped in cheap "westerns" and detective stories but trapped by the very nature of life itself. Sartre denies, on the one hand, that there are any meanings anywhere except those which man himself creates; on the other hand, in all his writings, philosophical or otherwise, he implies a givenness, if not a structure, to existence which is forever defeating man and his meanings. Meanings and values are, therefore, fragile, tentative, arbitrary, precarious. Although he affirms self-consciousness and the freedom of consciousness to create meanings, he insists that there would be no consciousness if it were not for the world outside consciousness. Between consciousness and the external world there is a sharp cleft which can never be overcome. And since the external world includes other objects endowed with consciousness and freedom, namely, other persons, alienation is deepest on the human level because the most formidable threat to a person is a person, not a thing. Only another person can penetrate my consciousness, thereby limiting, perhaps perverting, and even destroying me.

All this can be seen in Sartre's play, *No Exit*. Two women and a man are one by one ushered into a stuffy Victorian room, and the realization gradually comes that they are in hell. Inez admits at once that she is in the "right" place, but Estelle and Garcin try to pose as misplaced persons. Eventually, their defences are destroyed and each stands naked before the other. Then they begin to wonder when the torturer will come, and what form the torture will take. As they wait they begin to irritate each other as if by an inexorable compulsion. Estelle's earthly desires continue unabated; Inez is hard and brittle—"a dead twig, ready for the burning"; but Garcin died a coward, and this ignominy he can't shake off. As the mutual bedeviling mounts to the point of violence, Garcin makes a wild attempt to crash the bolted door, but there's NO EXIT. As they face the fact that there is no escape from each other, the horrible truth becomes clear—their torture consists in their condemnation to torture each other forever and ever and ever, and they break out in the laughter of the damned. As Garcin summarizes their situation the reader perceives that this is Sartre's summary of the human situation, per se: "So this is hell. I'd never believed it. You remember all we were told about the torture-chambers, the fire and brimstone, the 'burning marl.' Old wives' tales! There's no need for red-hot pokers. *Hell is—other people!*" [21] (Italics mine.)

The atheism of Sartre is primarily an inference from his view of man whose glory as well as his damnation is his freedom. There is not a more stalwart defender of human liberty than Sartre. Self-consciousness is freedom to make decisions, even though many decisions are nullified by external circumstances. To posit God as "Determiner of Destiny" would be to endanger human freedom, and this Sartre resolutely refuses to do—but not without a discernible wistfulness. For a man in his decision-making has no guides, no norms, no standards, and only the abyss below. Sartre finds it "very distressing that God does not exist, because all possibility of finding values in a heaven of ideas disappears along with Him; there can no longer be an *a priori* good, since there is no infinite and perfect consciousness to think it." The "forlornness" of men is rooted in their recognition "that God does not exist and that [they] have to face all the consequences of this." [22]

And what appears in the consciousness of a man who, having exercised his decision-making liberty in a godless world, stands at the brink of death? Listen to Pablo, the principal character in Sartre's short story entitled "The Wall," as he reflects upon his

[21] *No Exit* (New York: Vintage Books, 1955), pp. 46-47.
[22] *Existentialism* (New York: Philosophical Library, 1947), pp. 25-26.

predicament during the night preceding his scheduled execution at dawn: "At that moment I felt that I had my whole life in front of me and I thought, 'It's a damned lie.' It was worth nothing because it was finished. . . . I had spent my time counterfeiting eternity, I had understood nothing. . . . Death had disenchanted everything." [23] In his reflection upon his fate, Pablo's isolation is absolute. As Ignazio Silone so well says, "He who has faith is never alone. But the atheist is always alone, even if from morning to night he lives in crowded streets. The soul that does not know God is a leaf detached from the tree, a single, solitary leaf, that falls to the ground, dries up, and rots." [24]

Such is the bleak prospect of life without essential meaning (i.e., without God) as depicted by Eliot (from the perspective of the Christian faith), by Kafka (from the perspective of the residual religiousness of renounced Judaism), and by Sartre (from the perspective of declared atheism). It is a prospect envisioned by Nietzsche, who as early as 1882 wrote: "Is there any up or down left? Are we not straying as through an infinite nothing? Do we not feel the breath of empty space? Has it not become colder? Is not night and more night coming on all the while? Must not lanterns be lit in the morning?" [25] It is a prospect expressed succinctly by the Russian poet Tiutchev:

> Behold man, without home,
> orphaned, alone, impotent,
> facing the dark abyss;
> all light and life
> are no more than a past dream, far away.
> And in this strange mysterious night
> he sees and knows a fatal heritage.[26]

[23] Walter Kaufman (ed.), *Existentialism from Dostoevsky to Sartre* (New York: Meridian Books, 1956), p. 234.

[24] *Bread and Wine* (New York: Penguin Books, 1946), p. 82.

[25] Walter Kaufman (ed.), *The Portable Nietzsche* (New York: Viking Pr., 1954), p. 95.

[26] Quoted by Nicholas Berdyaev in *The End of Our Time* (New York: Sheed and Ward, 1933), p. 72.

What does this prospect have to do with vocation? Just this: Only when men believe in God can they perceive substantial meaning in existence; only when men can perceive meaning can they be captivated by vocation; and when men are captivated by vocation, they can live above despair to the glory of God.

It should be noted, however, that no attempt is being made to defend the thesis that the contemporary phenomenon of meaninglessness can be explained simply in terms of the decay of a dynamic concept of vocation. The roots of meaninglessness are deep, diverse, and devious. What is being affirmed is that the Christian understanding of vocation is tremendously relevant to the problem of meaninglessness in culture as a whole, in commerce and industry, in other occupational fields, and in community relationships. The picture painted by Eliot, Kafka, and Sartre probably appears extravagant to the average American, but he certainly recognizes some evidences of meaninglessness around him and within his own life—at least enough to appreciate the thrust of the epigram attributed to Toyohiko Kagawa.

> I read
> In a book
> That a man called
> Christ
> Went about doing good.
> It is very disconcerting to me
> That I am so easily
> Satisfied
> With just
> Going about—

Just going about—that is life without vocation. And that is a far cry from what God the Father of our Lord Jesus Christ intended human life to be!

When "just going about" becomes a burden to man sometimes he perceives that his only way out is to keep an Appointment. This seems to be the meaning, or at least one of the meanings, of

Samuel Becket's controversial play, *Waiting for Godot*.[27] The principal characters, Vladimir and Estragon, have a vague sense that there is an Appointment which they must keep, and so they wander around aimlessly waiting for Godot. As they wait they hear a cry for help from a chance wayfarer. Vladimir feels a tug to respond. "It is not every day that we are personally needed," he says to Estragon. "Let us make the most of it before it is too late." But they don't go to the help of Pozzo. Somehow they are powerless to respond until Godot comes. As they sink into a stupor of boredom and frustration, Vladimir soliloquizes—

Tomorrow, when I wake, or think I do, what shall I say of today? That with Estragon, my friend, at this place, until the fall of night, I waited for Godot? That Pozzo passed, with his carrier, and that he spoke to us? Probably. But in all that what truth will there be? (Estragon, having struggled with his boots in vain, is dozing off again. Vladimir looks at him.) He'll know nothing. He'll tell me about the blows he received and I'll give him a carrot. (Pause.) . . . But habit is a great deadener. (He looks again at Estragon.) At me too some-one is looking, at me too someone is saying, He is sleeping, he knows nothing, let him sleep on.[28]

Indeed, Someone is looking at Everyman, but he is not saying, "sleep on." On the contrary, he is calling Everyman to waken from the stupor of boredom, or of meaningless wandering, to a new life swept clean by his Spirit and empowered with a mission to fulfil in his kingdom.

[27] New York: Grove Pr., 1954.
[28] *Ibid.*, pp. 58-59.

2

VOCATION ACCORDING TO
THE SCRIPTURES

Our exploration of the meaning of vocation must begin with the Bible. There is no other place to begin. As everyone knows, the Bible can be quoted to establish almost any point of view, to prove almost any proposition! This feat can be accomplished either by design or by inadvertence simply by quoting out of context or by dealing with only a segment of the biblical material. In our search for the meaning of vocation, therefore, we shall attempt to see the Bible "steadily and to see it whole."

According to the Scriptures, vocation is basically corporate. God calls a people. In the Old Testament this people, this community is Israel; in the New Testament, this people, this community is the church. The corporate vocation of the people of God is the context within which an individual is called, has a vocation.

In the Old Testament the Hebrew *qahal* is used to designate the assembly or the congregation of Israel, i.e., the people God has summoned or called together for his service. The Septuagint usually translates *qahal* into the Greek *ekklesia*, which originally had the purely secular meaning of the summoned citizenry but to which the Septuagint gave a definitely religious connotation. The early Christians, in turn, took over the word *ekklesia* to designate those called into fellowship with Christ, i.e., the church. The root of *ekklesia* is the noun *klesis*, meaning the call or the calling, and the verb *kalein*, meaning to call or to summon. The Hebrew *qahal*, then, and the Greek *ekklesia* convey the idea of

21

a people summoned or called for a particular purpose. The
summons may be in terms of a call to fellowship or feasting, to
a task or a responsibility, to a judgment or an accounting. *Klesis,*
therefore, has connotations of joy, of labor, and of discipline.

Vocation in the Old Testament

The theme of the drama of the Old Testament is "God and
His People." There are only two major roles, that of God and
that of Israel. God, being God, always knows his lines; but
Israel, being finite and sinful, forgets her. lines and must be
prompted constantly from the wings of the stage of history. The
prompters are the "judges," the priests, and the prophets—
especially the prophets.

A synopsis of the drama might read somewhat as follows:
God, who has a purpose he wishes to achieve, calls a people into
existence to carry out his purpose. He begins millenia ago by
making a covenant with Abraham; by renewing it with Isaac
and with Jacob; and finally by sealing it with the self-conscious
community of Israel. His purpose is, through Israel, to bless all
the inhabitants of the earth. Within the community of Israel
each person has a responsibility to perform whether it be that
of king or soldier or craftsman or shepherd. From time to time
God calls men and women from their ordinary responsibilities
to carry out special missions on behalf of his people. And so
Hosea is called from farming to remind Israel of her unfaithfulness, Isaiah from court duties to warn the Kingdom of Judah
against foreign entanglements, and Jeremiah from his priestly family obligations to lay upon the people of Jerusalem the demands of
righteousness as over against the futility of formalized religion.
Despite the faithfulness of God to the covenant, Israel's persistent
unfaithfulness leads to disaster after disaster until only a remnant
remains. And out of this remnant, which still remembers the

vocation of Israel, eventually comes the Messiah. Now let us take a look at some of the detail of this drama.

1. *It is God, as the Lord of history, who takes the necessary steps to lay the foundations of a community with a unique destiny.*

It was customary for Israel to push back her covenant relationship to the era of the patriarchs. God summons Abram in Haran, and makes a covenant with him: "Go . . . and I will bless you . . . and I will bless those who bless you . . . and by you all the families of the earth will bless themselves" (Gen. 12:1-3). He renews the covenant with Isaac: "I will multiply your descendants . . . and by your descendants all the nations of the earth shall bless themselves, because Abraham obeyed my voice and kept my charge . . ." (Gen. 26:4-5). He renews the covenant with Jacob: "I am the Lord, the God of Abraham your father and the God of Isaac . . . and by you and your descendants shall all the families of the earth bless themselves. . . . Behold, I am with you and will keep you wherever you go . . ." (Gen. 28:13-15; cf. 35:10-12 and 46:2-4). Although the divine summons is here addressed to individuals, the emphasis is upon the continuing people of God and their role among all the families of the earth. The saga of Abraham, Isaac, and Jacob is of the nature of a prologue to the main action of the drama.

At every step the initiative rests with God. Abraham does not, for example, after due reflection, devise and promote a five-hundred-year plan whereby his descendants would greatly prosper and would shape the course of history. Rather, God lays hold of men, issues orders, and demands obedience; and men respond in trust.

2. *Through rescue and discipline God creates a community conscious of and dedicated to a unique destiny.*

Until the delivery from bondage in Egypt the people of Israel give little evidence of a sense of high destiny. Although such a sense of destiny is attributed to the patriarchs, one gets the impression that it was not shared by their numerous offspring and their respective families. And certainly there is no evidence of a sense of high destiny among the miserable Hebrew slaves under the whips of their Egyptian taskmasters. A dramatic rescue and re-creation had to take place, and for this purpose God called Moses to a special mission.

The call of Moses is one of the classic accounts in the Old Testament of human reaction to divine summons (Exod. 3-4). First, something had to happen to break the thread of routine experience before Moses decided to "turn aside." Only after he had turned aside to gaze at the burning bush could he hear the voice, "Moses, Moses," to which he replied, "Here am I." And the voice continued: "I am the God of your father, the God of Abraham, the God of Isaac, and the God of Jacob. . . . I have seen the affliction of my people who are in Egypt . . . and I have come down to deliver them. . . . Come, I will send you to Pharaoh that you may bring forth my people, the sons of Israel, out of Egypt." Instead of feeling himself highly honored, Moses is dismayed, and offers all sorts of excuses: I have no credentials; no one will believe me; I am not a good speaker. Only after every objection has been answered does Moses capitulate.

Interesting and significant as the call of Moses may be, its significance is only derivative. The primary call is the summons to Israel. "When Israel was a child, I loved him, and out of Egypt I called my son" (Hos. 11:1; cf. Exod. 4:22-23). God called Israel out of Egypt through Moses. The divine objective was the deliverance of Israel, not the deliverance of Moses from the tedium of sheep-grazing for his father-in-law!

The story of Israel's delivery from Egypt and the discipline in the desert needs no retelling. For our purposes it is sufficient to note that the biblical account of these forty years throws much light upon the Hebrew concept of vocation. Out of long and bitter experience Israel's understanding of her vocation was developed and strengthened. One of the finest descriptions of this vocation is in Deuteronomy 7:6-8:

> You are a people holy to the Lord your God; the Lord your God has chosen you to be a people for his own possession, out of all the peoples that are on the face of the earth. It was not because you were more in number than any other people that the Lord set his love upon you and chose you, for you were the fewest of all peoples; but it is because the Lord loves you, and is keeping the oath which he swore to your fathers, that the Lord has brought you out with a mighty hand, and redeemed you from the house of bondage, from the hand of Pharaoh, king of Egypt.

At Sinai the covenant is spelled out on the human side in the magnificent and ageless terms of the Decalogue (Exod. 20:1-17; cf. Deut. 5:6-21). It is to be noted that these obligations of Israel were not determined around a bargaining table with the Senior Member of the covenant, but were the conditions prescribed by the Lord, who said in effect: If I am to be your God and you are to be my people, you cannot do this and this and this! Or to put it positively, "And now, Israel, what does the Lord your God require of you, but to fear the Lord your God, to walk in all his ways, to love him, to serve the Lord your God with all your heart and with all your soul, and to keep the commandments and statutes of the Lord" (Deut. 10:12-13; cf. also vss. 14-22).

In the biblical account of the forty years in the desert there is the recognition that within the vocation of Israel are not only the special tasks of a Moses or an Aaron but also the special tasks of craftsmen. The instructions for the building of the tabernacle and its equipment contain such illuminating passages as the following: "The Lord said to Moses, 'See, I have called by name Bezalel the son of Uri, son of Hur, of the tribe of Judah: and I have filled him with the Spirit of God, with ability and intelligence, with knowledge and all craftsmanship, to devise artistic designs, to work in gold, silver, and bronze, in cutting stones for setting, and in carving wood, for work in every craft.

And behold I have appointed with him Oholiab, the son of
Ahisamach, of the tribe of Dan; and I have given to all able
men ability, that they may make all that I have commanded
you" (Exod. 31:1-6; cf. 35:30-35). "And all women who had
ability spun with their hands, and brought what they had spun
in blue and purple and scarlet stuff and fine twined linen; and
all the women whose hearts were moved with ability spun the
goats' hair" (Exod. 35:25). It is to be noted that these men and
women practiced their crafts in the ordinary day-by-day life of
the community, but here they are being called to special tasks
to help advance the spiritual life of the people by the provision
of a sanctuary.

The covenant with Israel involved both corporate and individual responsibilities. It is significant that the Decalogue was
addressed to Israel as a community but the response of obedience
involved the individual members of the community. In other
words, the call of Israel placed upon every Israelite the obligation of playing his proper role in the consecrated community, of
dedicating his whole being to the service of Israel's God. To
which tasks each member of the community should give himself,
however, was not a matter of special divine revelation. It is
true that in the case of the priesthood the whole tribe of Levi
was set aside for this purpose (Num. 1:47-50; cf. 8:14ff). Otherwise, variable tribal traditions and the possession of certain skills
apparently determined the occupations which the Israelites followed and which provided their tithes and offerings to the Lord.
The element of personal choice was probably very small indeed,
and, of course, nonexistent in conscription for the army and for
certain other types of service to the nation.

Although there is no evidence that shepherds and carpenters
and masons felt themselves to be divinely called to those particular
occupations, it was generally recognized that success in all labor
depended ultimately upon the divine favor. As the psalmist
puts it (127:1):

Hosea, following Amos (746-743 B.C.), also condemns Israel in terms of her unfaithfulness to the God who loved her and ransomed her out of slavery.

> Rejoice not, O Israel!
> Exult not like the peoples;
> for you have played the harlot, forsaking your God.
> > You have loved a harlot's hire
> > upon all threshing floors. (9:1)

> My God will cast them off,
> > because they have not hearkened to him;
> > they shall be wanderers among the nations. (9:17)

Micah, a man of the people, denounces both kingdoms (739-701 B.C.) for claiming God's protection without meeting the demands of justice.

> Hear this, you heads of the house of Jacob
> > and rulers of the house of Israel,
> who abhor justice
> > and pervert all equity,
> who build Zion with blood
> > and Jerusalem with wrong.
> Its heads give judgment for a bribe,
> > its priests teach for hire,
> > its prophets divine for money;
> yet they lean upon the Lord and say,
> > "Is not the Lord in the midst of us?
> > No evil shall come upon us."
> Therefore because of you
> > Zion shall be plowed as a field;
> Jerusalem shall become a heap of ruins,
> > and the mountain of the house a wooded height. (3:9-12)

Isaiah, a member of the aristocracy, delivers warnings to Judah (739-701 B.C.) to eschew foreign alliances and to take God seriously as her only counselor and protector.

"Woe to the rebellious children," says the Lord,
"who carry out a plan, but not mine;
and who make a league, but not of my spirit,
    that they may add sin to sin;
who set out to go down to Egypt,
    without asking for my counsel,
to take refuge in the protection of Pharaoh,
    and to seek shelter in the shadow of Egypt!" (30:1-2)

Hear, O heavens, and give ear, O earth;
    for the Lord has spoken:
"Sons have I reared and brought up,
    but they have rebelled against me.
The ox knows its owner,
    and the ass its master's crib;
but Israel does not know,
    my people does not understand." (1:2-3)

Jeremiah, after the collapse of the Northern Kingdom, pleads
in vain (625-586 B.C.) with Jerusalem to avoid a similar fate, but
foresees a saving remnant and a new covenant.

"Hear the word of the Lord, O nations,
    and declare it in the coastlands afar off;
say, 'He who scattered Israel will gather him,
    and will keep him as a shepherd keeps his flock.' " (31:10)

"Behold, the days are coming, says the Lord, when I will make a
new covenant with the house of Israel and the house of Judah, not
like the covenant which I made with their fathers when I took them
by the hand to bring them out of the land of Egypt, my covenant
which they broke, though I was their husband, says the Lord. But
this is the covenant which I will make with the house of Israel after
those days, says the Lord: I will put my law within them, and I will
write it upon their hearts; and I will be their God, and they shall be
my people." (31:31-33)

To recapitulate the vocational guidance as addressed to Israel
by the prophets: God called you into a covenant relationship with

himself to the end that through you all people would be blessed; this call conferred no immunity to difficulties or even to disaster in case you failed to keep the covenant; and so your unfaithfulness has brought punishment, designed for your purification; out of this crucible of fire a remnant will be saved, through which God's purposes will yet be realized.

Within the vocation of Israel the prophets were called to perform their special assignments, just as Moses had received a special call. In the Old Testament "the call experience" of these men is at times only intimated and at other times described in detail. With reference to the latter category, the stories of the call of Moses (Exod. 3-4), of Samuel (I Sam. 3), of Isaiah (chap. 6), and of Jeremiah (chap. 1) are well known. It is important to remember that these calls were not sought. In fact, they came as a surprise, indeed as a shock. Protestations of incompetence were met with assurances of divine help adequate to the assignment. These calls to special assignments were not regarded as a summons to greatness (i.e., to honor and acclaim) but rather to humble service. The carrying out of the special assignments usually plunged a person into both inner torment and outward persecution at the hands of those being served. Despite the torment and the abuse, however, there was no escaping such a call from the Holy One of Israel (cf. Ezek. 33:7-9 and the experience of Jonah).

This last observation is equally applicable to Israel herself. God laid his hand upon Israel to be his very own. In the long story of her vicissitudes, time and again she would have been glad to renounce her election. She tried turning a deaf ear to the divine summons, but to no avail (cf. Jer. 7:12-14 and Isa. 65:12). And so divine decimation would follow hard upon Israel's deviltry, but never to her complete obliteration. She could be carried into captivity, but even there she could not escape her divine Pursuer.

Such is vocation in the Old Testament: the calling of Israel to be God's people for the fulfilment of his purposes in the world.

This is the key to the meaning of history and to the meaning of
human existence itself. The call of God is both a wondrous and
an awesome thing. To be called is to come face to face with
great promise and with great peril. To respond in trust and
obedience is possible only by the grace of him who calls.

Vocation in the New Testament

Jeremiah and Isaiah saw Israel reduced to a mere "remnant,"
to which was entrusted the world's only remaining hope. And
out of this remnant came the Messiah, in whom were concen-
trated all the promises God had made to the chosen people. In
the words of the Magnificat,

> "He has helped his servant Israel,
> in remembrance of his mercy,
> as he spoke to our fathers,
> to Abraham and to his posterity forever."
> (Luke 1:54-55)

The culmination of the ancient promises is also affirmed in the
Benedictus.

> "Lord, now lettest thou thy servant depart in peace,
> according to thy word;
> for mine eyes have seen thy salvation
> which thou hast prepared in the presence of all peoples,
> a light for revelation to the Gentiles,
> and for glory to thy people Israel." (Luke 2:29-32)

The fact that Jesus chose twelve disciples (after the twelve
tribes) at the outset of his ministry indicates that he deliberately
intended to show the continuity between Israel's mission and his
mission, and that he saw his mission in relation to a community
identified with him. Although he did not specifically use the
term "remnant," it is clear that he saw his disciples as the nucleus

of a New Israel. "Fear not, little flock [remnant?], for it is your Father's good pleasure to give you the kingdom" (Luke 12:32).

After Pentecost the Christian community claimed explicitly to be the true Israel, the inheritor of all the promises made to the patriarchs. The outpouring of the Spirit is the fulfilment of the prophecy of Joel (Acts 2:17-21), and Jesus is vindicated as Israel's Messiah by the resurrection. All who repent and are baptized shall receive the blessing promised "to you and to your children, and to all that are far off, every one whom the Lord our God calls to him" (Acts 2:39). "You are the sons of the prophets and of the covenant which God gave to your fathers, saying to Abraham, 'And in your posterity shall all the families of the earth be blessed'" (Acts 3:25). The call of God, however, was still addressed primarily to the Jews, as was the case with the teaching and healing ministry of the Messiah himself. It can be said that at the outset both Jesus and his disciples regarded their mission as being first "to the lost sheep of the house of Israel" (Matt. 10:6).

Eventually it became evident that Israel as a whole had no intention of responding to the proclaimed Messiah. Because of this rejection, Paul declared that the call of God was now addressed to all people everywhere. The rejection by the old Israel and the constitution of the new Israel are worked out in a masterful but poignant fashion by Paul in his letter to the Romans. "But it is not as though the word of God had failed," he writes. "For not all who are descended from Israel belong to Israel, and not all are children of Abraham because they are his descendants; but 'Through Isaac shall your descendants be named.' This means that it is not the children of the flesh who are the children of God, but the children of the promise are reckoned as descendants" (Rom. 9:6-8). And thus the transition is made from the Israel bound together by blood relationship with Abraham to the Israel bound together by the Spirit in the body of Christ. The same God who called Israel into being has now called the church into being to carry out his purposes in the world.

With this brief historical sketch as a background, let us now look for further illumination of the concept of vocation in the New Testament.

1. *God takes the initiative to call men through the Holy Spirit into his fellowship to be a holy people, the communion of saints, the body of Christ, the* ekklesia.

God takes the initiative. He moves before men can anticipate their destiny; he acts according to his own purposes; he offers to bestow his gifts out of pure grace. Our Lord himself is reported in the Fourth Gospel as saying to his disciples, "You did not choose me, but I chose you and appointed you" (John 15:16). And the theme is taken up after Pentecost by the leaders of the church. In the letter to the Ephesians a Christian's calling is pushed back to "before the foundation of the world" when God "destined us in love to be his sons through Jesus Christ" (Eph. 1:4-6). The emphasis upon the divine initiative is especially strong in a well-known passage in Paul's letter to the Romans.

We know that in everything God works for good with those who love him, who are called according to his purpose. For those whom he foreknew he also predestined to be conformed to the image of his Son, in order that he might be the firstborn among many brethren. And those whom he predestined he also called; and those whom he called he also justified; and those whom he justified he also glorified (8:28-30; cf. 9:23-24, and II Thess. 2:13-15).

Other New Testament statements make the same point. In II Timothy 1:9 we read that God has "saved us and called us with a holy calling, not in virtue of our works but in virtue of his own purpose and the grace which he gave us in Christ Jesus." Likewise in II Peter 1:3: "His divine power has granted to us all things that pertain to life and godliness, through the knowledge

of him who called us to his own glory and excellence, by which
he has granted to us his precious and very great promises."

Furthermore, God calls men not into a "unilateral" relationship with him but into a corporate relationship, and this gives
them a corporate vocation. "You are a chosen race, a royal
priesthood, a holy nation, God's own people, that you may
declare the wonderful deeds of him who called you out of darkness into his marvelous light. Once you were no people but
now you are God's people" (I Pet. 2:9-10). Men are called into
unity with Christ and with each other; they "share in a heavenly
call," as the author of Hebrews puts it (3:1). The calling is not
a private possession. Again we must turn to Paul for a classical
statement of this truth.

For just as the body is one and has many members, and all the
members of the body, though many, are one body, so it is with Christ.
For by one Spirit we were all baptized into one body—Jews or
Greeks, slaves or free—and all were made to drink of one Spirit. For
the body does not consist of one member but of many. . . . If one
member suffers, all suffer together; if one member is honored, all
rejoice together. Now you are the body of Christ and individually
members of it (I Cor. 12:12-14, 26-27).

2. *The Holy Spirit calls men to different functions in the body
of Christ as God has bestowed upon them his gifts.*

The New Testament records specific instances where men
were called to special tasks within the community of faith. Jesus
himself not only called the twelve "to be with him" (Mark
1:16-20; 3:13-19) but he also sent them out to preach and to
heal (Luke 9:1-6; cf. Mark 6:7-13). Special assignments were
also made within the circle of the twelve. Peter, James, and
John constituted an inner circle, and performed certain extraordinary roles, such as accompanying Jesus up to the mount of
transfiguration (Matt. 17:1-8). Peter appears to be the chief
spokesman for the twelve, as for example in the conversation on
the way to Caesarea Philippi about the messiahship of Jesus

(Mark 8:27-30). Even Judas was given the special task of treasurer of the little group (John 13:29).

Paul frequently refers to his own call to be an apostle: "Paul, a servant of Jesus Christ, called to be an apostle, set apart for the gospel of God . . ." (Rom. 1:1; cf. Gal. 1:15). Within his call to the apostleship Paul was also called to particular places at particular times. Sometimes the call came through the church: "While they were worshiping the Lord and fasting, the Holy Spirit said, 'Set apart for me Barnabas and Saul for the work to which I have called them.' Then after fasting and praying they laid their hands on them and sent them off" (Acts 13:2-3). Sometimes the call came directly: "And a vision appeared to Paul in the night: a man of Macedonia was standing beseeching him and saying, 'Come over to Macedonia and help us.' And when he had seen the vision, immediately we sought to go on into Macedonia, concluding that God had called us to preach the gospel to them" (Acts 16:9-10). On the basis of his own experience and the experience of the whole Christian community Paul develops what might be called a theology of callings (services) within the church.

Now there are varieties of gifts, but the same Spirit; and there are varieties of service, but the same Lord; and there are varieties of working, but it is the same God who inspires them all in every one. To each is given the manifestation of the Spirit for the common good. To one is given through the Spirit the utterance of wisdom, and to another the utterance of knowledge according to the same Spirit, to another faith by the same Spirit, to another gifts of healing by the one Spirit, to another the workings of miracles, to another prophecy, to another the ability to distinguish between spirits, to another various kinds of tongues, to another the interpretation of tongues. All these are inspired by one and the same Spirit, who apportions to each one individually as he wills. . . . And God has appointed in the church first apostles, second prophets, third teachers, then workers of miracles, then healers, helpers, administrators, speakers in various kinds of tongues (I Cor. 12:4-11, 28).

Does the New Testament affirm that God directly calls men into secular occupations? Let us examine the principal passage, namely, I Corinthians 7:17-24, which is frequently interpreted to support the view that God calls men to be engineers in the same way that he called Paul to be an apostle.

Let every one lead the life which the Lord has assigned to him, and in which God has called him. This is my rule in all the churches. Was anyone at the time of his call already circumcised? Let him not seek to remove the marks of his circumcision. Was anyone at the time of his call uncircumcised? Let him not seek circumcision. For neither circumcision counts for anything nor uncircumcision, but keeping the commandments of God. Every one should remain in the state in which he was called. Were you a slave when called? Never mind. But if you gain your freedom, avail yourself of the opportunity. For he who was called in the Lord as a slave is a freedman of the Lord. Likewise he who was free when called is a slave of Christ. You were bought with a price; do not become slaves of men. So, brethren, in whatever state each was called, there let him remain with God.

Paul goes on to say, in connection with the question of whether or not to marry, that he is giving this counsel to remain in a present state because "the appointed time has grown very short" (I Cor. 7:29). Changing status is hardly worth the trouble since very soon all earthly status will disappear at the Parousia. Remain in your present state if at all possible and serve God there in keeping with his heavenly calling.

The key verses are 17, 20, and 24, and they have been variously interpreted. In the Revised Standard Version it is clear that the translators took the position that the calling referred to in the text is the calling of God in Christ to be his own people. This calling comes to men in all stations in life, in all types of situations— slave and free, circumcised and uncircumcised, married and unmarried. A man who hears the divine calling and responds should remain where he is, and live a life worthy of his calling into a new relationship with God in the church. The translators of the King James Version seem to have taken a different position, namely, that calling means both (a) the calling of God into fellowship and (b) the believer's station in life.

It can be argued that the Revised Standard Version translators have taken some liberty with the text inasmuch as in verse 20 the noun *klesis* is translated "state" while the verb form *kalein* is translated "called." The King James Version translators have, on the other hand, used "calling" and "called," respectively, to translate the two words. Technically, this may be a valid objection, but the King James Version, nevertheless, does violence to Pauline thought (and, indeed, to New Testament thought) as a whole.

Note should be taken that I Corinthians 7:20 is the only instance in the entire New Testament where *klesis* seems to indicate station or status in the world. In every other case it is used to describe the action of God in bringing man into fellowship with him or in summoning a person for a particular task in the church. It must be said, therefore, that I Corinthians 7:17-24 does not equate calling with occupation, at least in the strict sense. Granting for the moment that *klesis* is used in verse 20, its reference in the context is to marriage, slavery, and circumcision—not to carpentry or weaving! Paul gives no indication that he regarded tent-making as a calling. His calling was to sainthood and apostleship.

Let it be said at once, however, that the value and necessity of secular work are affirmed in the New Testament. Jesus himself worked as a carpenter before he began his public ministry (Mark 6:3) thus dignifying manual labor. Paul made tents for a living even after he launched upon his ministry (Acts 18:3) so that (a) his motivation for preaching the gospel could not be questioned and (b) he would not be a burden. So he writes to the Thessalonians: "You remember our labor and toil, brethren; we worked night and day, that we might not burden any of you, while we preached to you the gospel of God" (I Thess. 2:9). A Christian should work to provide not only for his own needs but also for those of his relatives and his brothers in the faith. "If anyone does not provide for his relatives, and especially for his own family, he has disowned the faith and is worse than an unbeliever" (I Tim. 5:8). Idleness is a sin against God and the community; in fact, "if anyone will not work, let him not eat" (II Thess. 3:10-12). Christians should be "ready for any honest work" (Titus 3:1). And their work should be so done that they "may command the respect of outsiders" (I Thess. 4:11-12).

The primary motivation of the Christian in his daily work, however, is not to make a good impression upon those outside the household of faith. Christians should rather do their work "not in the way of eyeservice, as men-pleasers, but as servants of Christ" (Eph. 6:5-9). For a Christian's whole life, including his labors, comes under this injunction: "Whatever you do, in word or deed, do everything in the name of the Lord Jesus" (Col. 3:17; cf. I Cor. 10:31).

It must be admitted, however, that the vast majority of statements in the New Testament concerning work unmistakably refer to work in the church or of the church, namely, ministering to the household of believers and bringing others into that household. The much-quoted phrase "fellow-workers for God" (I Cor. 3:9; cf. Rom. 16:9) clearly refers not to secular employment but to the work of making Christ known. And the same is true of Paul's well-known appeal to the Corinthians to stand firm "always abounding in the work of the Lord, knowing that in the Lord your labor is not in vain" (I Cor. 15:58). That there are valid implications in these passages for all work cannot be denied, and these will be considered at a later point in these lectures, but now we are concerned only to understand what the Scriptures do or do not say on the subject of vocation.

3. *In Christ God calls his people to a life of sanctification, whatever their station may be, in obedience to the Holy Spirit.*

The people of God are "called to be saints together with all those who in every place call on the name of our Lord Jesus Christ, both their Lord and ours" (I Cor. 1:2). This label "saints," frequently applied in the New Testament to members of the body of Christ, does not, of course, mean that the bearers are free from sin! On the contrary, a Christian is *simul justus et peccator* (at the same time justified and a sinner), and remains so until the end of this age. Rather are the saints (*hagioi*) summoned to be "separated" from the world, not in geographical isolation but in their nonconformity to merely secular norms. "Do not be conformed to this world but be transformed by the renewal of your mind, that you may prove what is the will of God, what is good and acceptable and perfect" (Rom. 12:2). A man is a saint by the grace of God, but he is expected to grow in grace, "to mature manhood, to the measure of the stature of the fulness of Christ" (Eph. 4:13).

The New Testament is full of exhortations to those who have been called into the body of Christ to be worthy of that calling. *The whole life of the Christian becomes, therefore, part and parcel of his vocation under God.* Having been bought with a price, he lays his whole being upon the altar in complete dedication to his Creator and Redeemer. "To this end we always pray for you," writes Paul to the Thessalonians, "that our God may make you worthy of his call, and may fulfil every good resolve and work of faith by his power, so that the name of our Lord Jesus may be glorified in you, and you in him" (II Thess. 1:11-12).

A Christian's life is rooted and grounded in the life of the community of believers. First of all, then, his vocation has certain implications for his relationships within the community. It is essential that in the church he must "lead a life worthy of the calling to which [he has] been called" (Eph. 4:1). In fact, most of the exhortations to live a life consistent with one's calling have as their point of application the household of faith even though many of them are quoted today in preaching and teaching within a much wider context. The original intention must not be forgotten, however, because unless Christians take their calling seriously within the church there is not much hope of their taking it seriously in the world outside the church.

Although a Christian's life is rooted and grounded in the community of believers, most of his life, quantitatively speaking, is lived in the world. Consequently, the vocation of a Christian has certain implications for his relationships outside the community. As noted above in the consideration of daily work, a Christian cannot be satisfied to do just as well in the world of work as nonbelievers; he must yet do more and more, he must go the second mile. The New Testament writers try to describe the meaning of this for Christians in various stations in life. The following quotation from I Peter (2:18-21) is merely illustrative: "Servants, be submissive to your masters with all respect, not only to the kind and gentle but also to the overbearing. For one is approved if, mindful of God, he endures pain while suffering unjustly. For what credit is it, if when you do wrong and are beaten for it you take it patiently? But if when you do right and suffer for it you take it patiently, you have God's approval. For to this you have been called, because Christ also suffered for you, leaving you an example, that you should follow in his steps."

These, in summary, are the meanings of vocation in the New Testament: (a) God calls men into the church through repentance and faith in Christ; (b) within the church he calls certain individuals to perform special functions; and (c) he calls all members of the body of Christ to a holy life in all their relationships. The similarity of these meanings to the meanings of vocation discovered in the Old Testament is obvious, and the similarity is not accidental.

Because God chose Israel to be his people, and delivered her out of bondage, he expected the Israelites to behave toward him, toward each other, and toward the world in a very special way, spelled out in terms of the law and sealed by a covenant. In like manner God has delivered us from bondage through Christ the Liberator, called us to be the new Israel, and expects us to behave toward him, toward each other, and toward the world in a very special way, spelled out in terms of faith active in love and sealed by the blood of a new covenant.

The overarching theme of both Testaments is the calling of the people of God—not "the flight of the alone to the Alone." This contrast draws attention to two distinctions: First, God, not man, takes the initiative. Second, persons in community, not individuals in isolation, is the divine goal. Vocation is, therefore, basically corporate; in a derivative sense it is also individual. There is only one calling of God, and this calling lays claim to a person's whole life both in the community of faith and in the world. This is vocation according to the Scriptures.

3

LUTHER'S UNDERSTANDING

OF VOCATION

The New Testament recognizes only one calling of God—a calling that redeems life in the body of Christ and that lays claim to life, to a person's whole life both in the community of faith and in the world. And so Paul writes to all the members of the church at Thessalonica: "We always pray for you, that our God may make you worthy of his call, and may fulfil every good resolve and work of faith by his power, so that the name of our Lord Jesus may be glorified in you" (II Thess. 1:11-12). Every Christian has a vocation!

Furthermore, in the New Testament the Christian life is portrayed as being in the world although not of it. There is no indication that Christians should withdraw from participation in the established social order, either by geographical segregation or by denying certain basic human functions and relationships.

Another point of view had appeared by the beginning of the fourth century. Eusebius, for example, writes about A.D. 315 as follows:

Two ways of life were thus given by the law of Christ to His Church. The *one* is above nature, and beyond common human living; it admits not marriage, child-bearing, property nor the possession of wealth, but, wholly and permanently separate from the common customary life of mankind, it devotes itself to the service of God alone in its wealth of heavenly love! . . . Such then is the perfect form of the Christian life. And the *other*, more humble, more

43

human, permits men to join in pure nuptials and to produce children, to undertake government, to give orders to soldiers fighting for right; it allows them to have minds for farming, for trade, and the other more secular interests as well as for religion; and it is for them that times of retreat and instruction, and days for hearing sacred things are set apart. *And a kind of secondary grade of piety is attributed to them* . . . (Italics mine).[1]

One can find no explicit reference to vocation; but now there are two classes of Christians—those who live "above nature" and those who remain in nature, living a "more human" life. This distinction having been made, there followed rapid growth of monasticism and of the belief that only celibate withdrawal from human society had the full approval of God.

Where Luther differed from Rome

By the fifteenth century the division between ordinary Christians and Christians seeking perfection had become complete. It meant a fatal recognition of a double standard of conduct and of responsibility: one for the monk, the nun, and the priest and the other for the believer who continued his activities in the everyday world. And the term "vocation" was applied only to the former. *Only the monk, the nun, and the priest had callings.* Christians in the secular world had no vocations.

And so it was that monasteries and convents played a central role in the life of the medieval church. Monks and nuns by separating themselves from the world gained positive merit both for themselves and for those who remained in the world. Life was a two-story affair with farmers, soldiers, and craftsmen on the ground level keeping the wheels of normal human life going, and with those committed to obedience, poverty, and celibacy on the second level with their eyes (supposedly) fixed upon heaven.

[1] Quoted by W. R. Forrester, *Christian Vocation* (New York: Scribner's, 1953), p. 43.

Against this stratification of Christendom, this sharp distinction between the secular and sacred, Luther rebelled. Man is not justified before God by what he does or does not do in relation to other men. Perfection is demanded of all men—not just of those in the cloister. And men, regardless of where they live, are all incapable of perfection. Monks are no better than masons in the sight of the High and Holy One. The salvation of both monks and masons depends entirely upon the unmerited grace of God shed abroad in Christ, the Savior.

Out of gratitude and love, insisted Luther, the Christian will gladly serve his fellows in whatever situation he finds himself, and with absolutely no expectation of reward either from God or man. Only a person liberated by Christ can afford to live like that! He can afford it because in Christ he has everything he needs for time and eternity. He can forget about merit. He can concentrate upon his brothers' needs.

Having rejected the basis for the medieval double standard of Christian living, Luther had two alternatives before him in regard to vocation: (a) he could proceed to deny the validity of vocation with reference to any station in life; or (b) he could extend vocation to include all stations in life, clerical and lay, "spiritual" and "secular." He chose the second alternative, and thereby ushered in a new era of understanding of and concern for Christian vocation in the Western world.

Luther's concept of vocation, like a coin, has two sides to it—but it is one coin! On one side he conceives of vocation as gospel, as a call to life in Christ and in his body, the church; on the other side he conceives of vocation as law, as a call to obedience and service.

One cannot understand Luther's concept of vocation without reference to his even more basic concept of the two kingdoms (realms): the kingdom of grace and the kingdom of creation. Both are God's kingdoms. And yet they must never be merged, and never be separated. Furthermore, they are co-ordinate realms: one cannot be subordinated to the other. The kingdom of grace is on the right hand; the kingdom of creation is on the left hand. The kingdom of grace is the realm of faith and of the freedom of the sons of God. The kingdom of creation is the realm where the believer serves God by serving his fellow human beings. In this realm men may co-operate with God, in faith, in the achievement of his purposes. God may also use men as his instruments even though they may not be aware of the role they are playing.

It is important and illuminating to note that Luther's concept of vocation is applicable to both kingdoms: God calls men into the kingdom of grace, where he bestows upon them forgiveness and fellowship, and he calls men to serve their fellows in the kingdom of creation. Just as both kingdoms belong to the one God, so do both the life of unmerited grace and the life of obedient service belong to one vocation.

Vocation as grace

God calls men through the Holy Spirit to a life of divine forgiveness and fellowship in the church. This primary understanding is clearly evident in Luther's explanation of the Third Article of the Creed in his Small Catechism.

I believe that I cannot by my own reason or strength believe in Jesus Christ, my Lord, or come to Him; but *the Holy Ghost has called (berufen) me by the gospel,* enlightened me with His gifts, sanctified and kept me in the true faith; *even as He calls (beruft), gathers, enlightens, and sanctifies the whole Christian Church* on earth, and keeps it with Jesus Christ in the one true faith; in which Christian Church He forgives daily and richly all sins to me and all believers, and at the last day will raise up me and all the dead, and will give to me and to all believers in Christ everlasting life. This is most certainly true (Italics mine).[2]

---

[2] *Triglot Concordia* (St. Louis: Concordia, 1921), pp. 544-45.

The reference to the calling of the church receives further support and elucidation in the Large Catechism, as follows:

> I believe that there is upon earth a little holy group and *congregation of pure saints,* under one head, even Christ, *called together* (*zukammen-berufen*) *by the Holy Ghost* in one faith, one mind, and understanding, with manifold gifts, yet agreeing in love, without sects or schisms. I am also a part and member of the same, a sharer and *joint owner* of all the goods it possesses (Italics mine).[3]

It is difficult to determine from these quotations whether Luther regarded the call in this primary sense as being basically individual or basically corporate. Within the whole context of Luther's writings we are warranted in affirming that Luther emphasized the divine call to the individual, but at the same time he recognized that there is no call apart from the church. Even as the calling together of the whole church goes on to the end of time, so the calling of individuals into the church goes on to the end of time. It is the same calling, looked at from different perspectives. As the Holy Spirit calls, enlightens, and sanctifies the church so he calls, enlightens, and sanctifies each and every believer.

Unless God called there would be no faith in Jesus Christ, there would be no church. Man cannot by his own reason or strength believe in Jesus Christ or come to him. God must and does take the initiative to bring faith into being, to bring the church into being. Limited by his finitude and sinfulness, man is otherwise doomed to a pitifully cramped and frustrating existence. He never knows how cramped and frustrating it is, however, until God draws near and calls him into an entirely different kind of existence. The divine call is, therefore, a divine gift, a manifestation of grace, the gospel extended to hapless man in the place where he is.

---

[3] *Ibid.,* pp. 690-91.

This, then, is the primary meaning of calling as understood by Luther. Without this understanding clearly established, misunderstanding of everything else he said on the subject is almost certain to follow.

Vocation as service

God continues to call those who embrace his offer of forgiveness and fellowship to a life of loving service in all their relationships. This understanding of vocation is a derivative, a corollary of the primary meaning.

It must be recognized that vocation as service bulks larger in Luther's writings than vocation as fellowship in the church. This weighting in favor of the derivative rather than the primary meaning of calling must be seen in the light of two considerations.

In the first place, it must be remembered that Luther's most frequent use of the term "vocation" was in polemical reaction to the use of the term in the Roman church. In rejecting completely Rome's restrictive use of the term, it was necessary for Luther to emphasize (even overemphasize) his new, evangelical understanding of vocation as being applicable to every believer.

Secondly, Luther used many other concepts and metaphors to depict the seeking, searching, probing activity of God in relation to his fallen creatures. For example, in a sermon for the First Sunday in Advent he interprets our Lord's entry into Jerusalem as signifying God's initiative toward the human soul. "This is what is meant by 'Thy King Cometh.' You do not seek him, but he seeks you. You do not find him, he finds you. For the preachers come from him, not from you; their sermons come from him, not from you; your faith comes from him, not from you; everything that faith works in you comes from him, not from you; and where he does not come, you remain outside." [4]

[4] "Church Postils," in J. N. Lenker (ed.), *The Precious and Sacred Writings of Martin Luther* (Minneapolis: Lutherans of All Lands Co., 1905), X, 27.

A word must be said about Luther's use of I Corinthians 7:17-24, especially verse 20: "Every one should remain in the state [*klesei*] in which he was called [*eklethe*]." Luther translates *klesei* as *Ruf* and *eklethe* as *berufen ist*. He usually uses *Stand* to signify station. Nevertheless, for all practical purposes Luther uses vocation (*Beruf*) to cover both calling into the church and calling in a station, with emphasis upon the second usage. Gustaf Wingren seems to be correct when he says that "Luther does not use *Beruf* or *vocatio* in reference to the work of a non-Christian. All have station (*Stand*) and office [*Amt* or *Stelle*], but *Beruf* is the Christian's earthly or spiritual work." [5] The reason why this distinction is not always maintained by Luther is because he was writing about and for Christians, who had both *Stand* and *Beruf*.

Let us now examine more closely Luther's understanding of vocation as loving service.

1. *Every Christian has a vocation in life because every believer has a station, and in every station there are opportunities for service.* Vocation includes the total life of a man—not simply his occupation. God calls a man to lay his whole life on the altar of dedication. Vocation involves all relationships.

A Christian is called to be a faithful husband; he is called to be a wise and understanding father; he is called to be a responsible citizen; he is called to be a good neighbor; just as he is called to be a competent carpenter. In fact, it is not necessary to have a job in the popular sense in order to have a vocation. A retired carpenter, stricken by illness and lying helpless in bed, still has a vocation from his Lord.

All this Luther makes quite clear in his sermon on the Gospel lesson for the day of St. John the Evangelist (John 21:19-24). On the basis of this passage he addresses some illuminating admonitions to those who feel they have no vocation.

[5] *Luther on Vocation*, trans. by Carl C. Rasmussen (Philadelphia: Muhlenberg Pr., 1957), p. 2.

You may reply: But how if I am not called? Answer: How is it possible that you are not called? You have always been in some state or station; you have always been a husband or wife, a boy or girl, or servant. Picture before you the humblest state. Are you a husband, and you think you have not enough to do in that sphere to govern your wife, children, domestics, and property so that all may be obedient to God and you do no one any wrong? . . . Again: Are you a son or daughter, and do you think you have not enough work with yourself, to continue chaste, pure, and temperate during your youth, obey your parents, and offend no one by word or deed? . . . Again: Are you a domestic servant, and do you think you would go idle if you were to serve your lord or mistress with all faithfulness as your station and orders require, and also keep your mouth under control as with a bridle? . . . And again: Are you a prince, a lord, spiritual or secular—who has more to do than you, in order that your subjects may do right, preserve peace, and wrong is done by no one? . . . See, as now no one is without some commission and calling, so no one is without some kind of work, if he desires to do what is right. Every one, therefore, is to take heed to continue in his calling, look to himself, faithfully do what is commanded him, and serve God and keep his commandments; then he will have so much to do that all time will be too short, all places too cramped, all resources of help too weak.[6]

Note the wide sweep of vocation in Luther's thought. Everything is included from a husband's governing his household, to a daughter's keeping herself chaste, to a servant's holding his tongue, to a prince ruling his realm. And note, furthermore, that Luther thinks of all these activities as in some sense "work," i.e., that which God expects of man. Therefore, Luther says: "If you are a student, mind your studies; if you are a maid, sweep the house; if you are a servant, care for the horses; etc." [7]—and in so doing you will be fulfilling your vocation in the world.

2. *Vocation is given structure by God through "orders" and "offices" which, because divinely decreed, serve good and neces-*

---

[6] "Church Postils," *op. cit.*, pp. 242-43.
[7] Quoted by George W. Forell in *Faith Active in Love* (New York: American Pr., 1954), p. 148.

sary purposes even though some of them may involve evil men and seemingly evil actions. The affirmation of divinely decreed orders and offices imparts a realism to Luther's understanding of vocation in the world and at the same time safeguards a Christian's conscience.

The three primary orders which God the Creator has provided are the family, the state, and the organized church, and every Christian belongs to all three orders. Luther identified, rather naively, the economic order with that of the family. These orders will stand until the end of the world. They are a part of the basic structure of human existence. Within these orders there are offices, which may change from time to time but while they are operative God works through them.

When faithful and dedicated men hold offices which enjoy God's blessing the requirements of these offices become the responsibility of God himself. For example, within the order of the state are many offices which require that the officeholders do things which Christians, motivated by love, are hesitant to do. There are "the offices of the sword" (especially the judge, the executioner, the soldier) which involve condemning people to death, executing criminals, or slaying human beings in battle. In regard to these offices Luther writes: "The sword is in itself right and is a divine and useful ordinance, which God will not have despised, but feared, honored, and obeyed, on pain of vengeance, as Paul says, in Romans xiii. For He has established two kinds of government among men. The one is spiritual; it has no sword. . . . The other is worldly government, through the sword, which aims to keep peace among men. . . ." [8] Therefore, a Christian who must use the sword in the fulfilment of his official duties can do so with a free conscience.

This does not mean that all actions of an officeholder are *ipso*

---

[8] *Works of Martin Luther*, Philadelphia Edition (Philadelphia: Holman-Muhlenberg, 1915-43, hereafter cited as *PE*), V, p. 39 ("Whether Soldiers, Too, Can Be Saved").

facto the actions of God and consequently defensible actions. It must not be forgotten that all officeholders are sinners and can pervert their true responsibilities. So Luther makes a careful distinction "between an occupation and the man who is in it, between a work and the doer of it. An occupation can be good and right in itself and yet bad and wrong if the man in the occupation . . . does not do his duty rightly." [9] In fact, "where is there an office or a work or any other thing so good that self-willed, wicked people do not abuse it?" [10]

Closely related to Luther's concept of orders and offices is that of the divine masks or *larvae*, through which God reveals himself. The Most High never reveals himself in his naked transcendence to men. Christ in his incarnation was a mask of God, and through this mask God made himself known, acted on man's behalf. A mask both conceals and reveals the Creator. And so it is that orders and offices and stations are also *larvae Dei* through which God is constantly confronting men with his will and his power.

Still another concept of Luther is that of man being a conduit or channel through which the love and power of God may flow. All good things come from above, and man in his vocation is merely an instrument through which the divine activity takes place. It is essential that man keep himself "open" as a channel through which the divine love and power may flow, and this is accomplished by God himself in Word and sacrament, in forgiveness and fellowship.

3. *Everything a Christian does in his vocation is for the sake of his fellows, for the sake of their spiritual, physical, moral, or cultural welfare.* In the broadest sense, a Christian is called to work for the common welfare, but he does this in very specific ways within the context of his own station in life. "A cobbler, a smith, a farmer, . . . by means of his own work or office must

[9] *Ibid.*, p. 34.
[10] *Ibid.*, p. 37.

benefit and serve every other, that in this way many kinds of work may be done for the bodily and spiritual welfare of the community, even as all the members of the body serve one another." [11]

A corollary of this thesis is that nothing a man does in his vocation has any relevance to his eternal salvation. Being a faithful husband, a wise and understanding father, a responsible citizen, a good neighbor, and a competent carpenter will not win a Christian any "extra points" in the celestial record book. His status in the kingdom of heaven is secured by grace alone. In Luther's own words, "Christ has done and accomplished everything for you, atoned for your sins, secured grace and life and salvation." [12]

Still another corollary is that a man in his vocation "need not do any work for God nor for the departed saints." With reference to God, he is complete in himself and needs absolutely nothing for himself; and with reference to "the departed saints," it is too late to do anything for them! God can use a Christian to bring his blessings to men but he does not himself need a Christian. And so Luther delivers a blunt warning: "If you find a work by which you benefit God or his saints or yourself and not your neighbor, know that such a work is *not* good." "Hence direct all the good you can do and your whole life to the end that it may be good; but it is good only when it is useful to other people." [13]

A Christian's vocation of service should not be one of grim duty, of sternly accepted obligation. Luther never ceases to remind his readers that service should flow freely, spontaneously from love, which is in turn the gift of God. He does this most beautifully, of course, in his "Treatise on Christian Liberty," in which he writes as follows: "Lo, this is a truly Christian life,

---

[11] *PE* II, 69 ("An Open Letter to the Nobility").
[12] "Church Postils," *op. cit.*, p. 36.
[13] *Loc. cit.* (Italics mine).

here faith is truly effectual through love; that is, it issues in works of the freest service cheerfully and lovingly done, with which a man willingly serves another without hope of reward, and for himself is satisfied with the fulness and wealth of his faith." [14] Luther's strong conviction that true service is always filled with joy is well summarized by Wingren: "Love does not think about doing works, it finds joy in people; and when something good is done for others, that does not appear to love as works but simply as gifts which flow naturally from love. . . . He who has the Holy Spirit knows it by the fact, among others, that in faith and gladness he fulfils his vocation. . . . Finding love is thus the same thing as finding both neighbor and vocation to be something in which one can live with joy." [15]

And what is the final test of the validity of a man's vocation in the world? Just this: "Christ at the last day will not ask how much you have prayed, fasted, pilgrimaged, done this or that for yourself, but how much good have you done to others, even the very least." [16]

4. *All service in vocation ranks the same with God, and Christians may with equal confidence hold the lowest and the highest offices, but certain offices in themselves are of greater significance than others.* Inasmuch as man can achieve no merit with God by virtue of his service in vocation, no office from the divine perspective can have an advantage over another. So long as an office serves the common welfare it is pleasing in God's sight, and should be held in honor by men as the work of God.

There are differences between offices, however, that cannot be denied. The qualifications demanded by various offices differ greatly, both in native ability and in training. These differences in turn result in distinctions in social status and financial compensation. Such distinctions will always exist in any society.

---

[14] *PE* II, 336.
[15] Wingren, *op. cit.*, pp. 43-44.
[16] *PE* I, 240 ("Treatise on Good Works").

More important are the differences in significance for the common welfare. Obviously, a ditchdigger makes a contribution of far less significance to the common welfare than does a physician or a mayor of a city. Making a scale of offices on the basis of their relative value to a community necessarily involves a good deal of subjectivity. It is interesting and illuminating to note how Luther rates some of the occupations of his day.

At the top of the list he places the office of pastor. "There is no dearer treasure, nor any more precious thing on earth or in this life than a real and faithful pastor or preacher." [17] This statement, it should be noted, does not make the office of the pastor superior to all others but it does deny that there is another office of greater significance. At other places, however, he does give the pastoral office "an edge" over all others, and that for two reasons: (a) other offices were "not purchased at so dear a price as the preaching office, with the blood and the death of the Son of God"; and (b) the pastoral office deals with matters of eternal consequence, whereas all other offices are concerned with "this temporal, transient life." [18] Nevertheless, he feels that the pastoral office does not require as great native gifts as do other offices, notably that of law.[19] Also, by exalting the pastoral office he does not intend to imply that "every man must train his child for this office, for not all the boys must become pastors. . . ." [20]

Next on the list Luther places teaching. He even admits that sometimes he cannot make up his mind whether preaching or teaching is the higher office. "I myself," he writes, "if I could leave the preaching office and other things, or had to do so, would not be so glad to have any other work as that of schoolmaster, or teacher of boys, for I know that this is the most

[17] PE IV, 146 ("A Sermon on Keeping Children in School").
[18] PE IV, 158.
[19] PE IV, 163.
[20] PE IV, 153.

useful, the greatest, and the best, next to the work of preaching. Indeed, I scarcely know which of the two is the better. . . ." Of one thing he is certain, namely, that "a diligent and pious school-teacher or master, or whoever it is that faithfully trains and teaches boys, can never be sufficiently rewarded, or repaid with any money." [21]

For third place Luther names "the office of worldly government," which he describes as "a glorious ordinance of God and splendid gift of God." [22] "It is a necessary office and rank, which we can no more do without than we can do without life itself, since without government this life cannot continue." [23] To those in the office of worldly government Luther pays this extraordinary tribute: "Just as a pious theologian and sincere preacher is called, in the realm of Christ, an angel of God, a savior, prophet, priest, servant, and teacher, so a pious jurist and true scholar can be called, in the worldly realm of the emperor, a prophet, priest, angel, and savior. . . . When I speak of the jurists, I do not mean only the Doctors of Laws, but the whole profession, including chancellors, secretaries, judges, advocates, notaries, and all who have to do with the legal side of government." [24]

Somewhat below the offices of pastor, teacher, and lawyer Luther places other offices for which he has a high regard, namely, that of physician, writer, secretary, and "scholars in the liberal arts." His list, of course, is not meant to be exhaustive.

5. *A Christian should rejoice that he has a vocation in the world, and should remain in his station rather than try to escape it.* As we have seen, in Luther's judgment the vast majority of stations in life are ordained of God, and pleasing to him. All such stations are not equally pleasant, but they can all bring blessings

[21] *PE* IV, 173-74.
[22] *PE* IV, 158.
[23] *PE* IV, 159.
[24] *PE* IV, 161.

to the believer's neighbors. To rebel against one's station in the world is a serious matter.

In his exposition of Psalm 111, Luther applies the first part of verse 4, "Full of honor and adornment is his work," to the stations of men.

This is a thanksgiving for all the works of God which He ordains among men, as, for example, the various situations, offices, and duties among men. Surely, anyone should laugh in his heart for joy if he finds himself in a station that God instituted or ordained. He ought to shout and dance as he thanks God for such a divine act, because here he hears and is assured that his position is full of honor and adornment before God. . . . Now, this means that a servant, maid, son, daughter, man, woman, lord, subject, or whoever else may belong to a station ordained by God, as long as he fills his station, is as beautiful and glorious in the sight of God as a bride adorned for her marriage or as the image of a saint decorated for a high festival.[25]

It is incomprehensible to Luther why "the blind and senseless world will not see this." On the contrary, the world "despises such stations so shamefully," complains Luther, "that it makes a pious heart bleed." [26]

Consequently, because of this prevalent attitude, people are always trying to escape their stations. "Is one married, then he praises the state of one who has no wife; has he none, then he praises the married state. Is he in a spiritual calling, then he likes the secular; is he in a secular calling, then he prefers the spiritual." [27] When a man will not accept his station, so that it comes within his vocation, there is little that God can do with him. "It is much to be lamented," says Luther in his *Table Talk*, "that no man is content and satisfied with that which God gives

[25] *Luther's Works*, American Edition (St. Louis: Concordia, 1956), XIII, 368.

[26] *Loc. cit.*

[27] "Church Postils," *op. cit.*, p. 246.

him in his vocation. . . . To serve God is for every one to remain in his vocation, . . . be it ever so mean and simple." [28]

Only if a man's station is inherently sinful should he abandon it. What does Luther mean by a station which is sinful in itself? Here is his answer:

> When I speak of a calling which in itself is not sinful, I do not mean that we can live on the earth without sin. All callings and estates sin daily; but I mean the calling God has instituted is not opposed to God, as for example, marriage, man-servant, maid-servant, lord, wife, superintendent, ruler, judge, officer, farmer, citizen, etc. I mention as sinful stations in life: robbery, usury, public women, and, as they are at present, the pope, cardinals, bishops, priests, monks and nuns, who neither preach nor listen to preaching.[29]

To be in an "irksome" station is one thing; to be in a sinful station is quite another thing. Blessed is he who can distinguish between the two, and acts accordingly.

6. *Inasmuch as all offices should be open to all qualified persons, education should be encouraged to the end that students may be adequately prepared for appropriate offices.* The one exception Luther made to this sweeping statement are the offices held by nobility and, therefore, filled on a hereditary basis.

His strong conviction that all offices should be open to properly qualified young persons considerably softens the hardness of his conviction that men should remain in the stations where God has placed them. Here is the chief passage which cracks the rigidity of the medieval pattern of stations.

> We ought to know that God is a wonderful lord. His trade is to take beggars and make them lords, just as He makes all things out of nothing. This trade of His no one will interfere with or hinder. He has the whole world sing of Him, in Psalm cxii, "Who is like the Lord, Who sitteth so high and beholdeth so deep? Who lifteth the

---

[28] *Luther's Table Talk*, trans. by William Hazlitt (Philadelphia: Lutheran Publication Society, 1873), p. 447.

[29] "Church Postils," *op. cit.*, p. 249.

small out of the dust and raiseth the poor out of the filth, that He may make them sit among the princes, even among the princes of His people." Look about you, at the courts of all the kings and princes, at the cities and the parishes; see whether this Psalm does not rule with many strong examples. There you will find jurists, doctors, counsellors, writers, preachers, who were usually poor and have certainly been boys at school, and have mounted and flown up by their pens (feathers), until they are lords, as the Psalm says, and like princes, help to rule lands and peoples. It is not God's will that born kings, princes, lords, and nobles should rule and be lords alone; He wills to have His beggars with them, so that they may not think that noble birth alone, and not God alone, makes lords and rulers.[30]

Therefore, Luther pleads that young persons be educated for the offices for which they have the proper talents. To parents he says: "If God has given you a child who has the ability and the talent for this office [i.e., pastor], and you do not train him for it, but look only to the belly and to temporal livelihood, see what a pious prig and small potato you are." [31] To the state he says: "I hold that it is the duty of the government to compel its subjects to keep their children in school, especially those children [with special abilities]. . . . Let the government, when it sees a promising boy, have him kept in school; if the father is poor, let it help him." [32] To the wealthy he says: "Let the rich make their wills with this work in view, as some have done who have endowed stipends; that is the right way to bequeath your money to the church. This way you do not, to be sure, release departed souls from purgatory, but by maintaining God's offices, you help the living and those to come who are not yet born." [33]

It must be remembered that in making this plea Luther was thinking of offices as being open to all men, Christians and non-

[30] *PE* IV, 171.
[31] *PE* IV, 151.
[32] *PE* IV, 177-78.
[33] *PE* IV, 178.

Christians presumably. For a Christian young person his office would be one segment of his total vocation under God.

It is time to pull together the strands of Luther's understanding of vocation. According to his understanding, God calls men through the Holy Spirit (a) to a life of divine forgiveness and fellowship in the church and (b) to a life of loving service in all human relationships. Luther focused attention upon vocation as loving service, and, therefore, as applicable to all Christians, because he was combatting the current Roman view that only monks, nuns, and priests had vocations.

In developing the concept of a Christian's vocation of service in the world, he affirmed six basic theses: (a) Every Christian has a vocation in the world because every Christian has a station in which he can serve his fellows. (b) Vocation in the world is given structure by means of divinely established orders and offices. (c) Everything a Christian does in his vocation in the world is for the sake of human welfare. (d) All service in vocation ranks the same with God but not all offices have the same significance in society. (e) A Christian should be grateful that he has a God-given vocation where he can remain in loving service. (f) All young persons should have opportunity to prepare for the offices for which they are best qualified.

Where Luther differed from Calvin

What are the similarities between Luther's concept of vocation and Calvin's concept of vocation? In the first place, Luther and Calvin would agree that a Christian's vocation in the world includes far more than his occupation, what he does for pay. Secondly, Luther and Calvin would agree that all stations in life, even the "mean and simple," enjoy the divine approbation. In the third place, Luther and Calvin would agree that a man may not lightly desert his station but should willingly serve at his post without complaint.

On the other hand, there are differences between Luther and Calvin, and these may be largely differences in emphasis. For Luther the primary reason why God gives a Christian a vocation in the world is to encourage a life of loving service whereas for Calvin the reason seems to be the proper ordering of human life, lest everything be thrown into confusion. It follows that in Calvin's understanding of vocation activity ought to be carefully calculated with a view to its propriety and effectiveness, whereas in Luther's understanding there is much room for spontaneity born of the dynamic of love which has its source in God. Consequently, in Calvin's view vocation affords great consolation whereas in Luther's view the divine blessing includes both consolation and unbounded joy. Finally, while Calvin sees vocation as a means of giving glory to God Luther sees it primarily as a means whereby God can bestow his good gifts upon men.

Some of the differences from Luther's concept of vocation which were implicit in Calvin's teachings became explicit in the Reformed tradition which developed after Calvin, especially at two points.

1. *In the Reformed tradition vocation is very closely related to predestination.* Vocation provides an excellent opportunity for a man to win assurance that he is among the elect, since God will certainly prosper the undertakings of those whom he has marked as his very own. In other words, confirm your election through your vocation! This view gains support from a passage in II Peter (1:3-11):

His divine power has granted to us all things that pertain to life and godliness, through the knowledge of him who called us to his own glory and excellence. . . . For this very reason make every effort to *supplement your faith* with virtue, and virtue with knowledge, and knowledge with self-control, and self-control with steadfastness, and steadfastness with godliness, and godliness with brotherly affection, and brotherly affection with love. . . . *Therefore, brethren, be the more zealous to confirm your call and election,* for if you do this you will never fall; so there will be richly provided for you an entrance into the eternal kingdom of our Lord and Savior Jesus Christ. (Italics mine.)

It should be noted that the believer is exhorted "to supplement" his faith, and that "entrance into the eternal kingdom" seems to be contingent upon the supplement! Calvinists made the most of this passage.

It is difficult to reconcile this interpretation of salvation and vocation with that of Luther. According to Luther, man in his vocation in the world can do nothing to secure his salvation, which is freely provided in Christ. In his secular vocation a Christian's entire attention is directed to his neighbor and his neighbor's welfare. Assurance of salvation (election) is sufficiently given in Word and sacrament.

2. *In the Reformed tradition vocation is a call to action, including what we now designate as "social action"*—the translation of the divine righteousness into the structures of human society. In contrast, Luther, on the whole, conceives of vocation in the world within the conventional limits of time-honored social patterns. As a result, the Lutheran interpretation of vocation tended to be quietistic while the Calvinist interpretation tended in the activist direction. What this meant for the Puritans is forcefully expressed by Tawney.

On the lips of the Puritan divines, [vocation] is not an invitation to resignation, but the bugle call which summons the elect to the long battle which will end only after death. "The world is all before them." They are to hammer out their salvation, not merely *in vocatione*, but *per vocationem*. The calling is not a condition in which an individual is born, but a strenuous and exacting enterprise, to be undertaken, indeed, under the guidance of Providence, but to be chosen by each man himself, with a deep sense of his solemn responsibilities.[34]

[34] *Religion and the Rise of Capitalism* (New York: Mentor Books, 1947), p. 200.

The fact that Luther was deeply suspicious of and bitterly opposed to the rising commercialism of his day, while Calvin recognized the burgeoning world of commerce as an area of legitimate activity for a Christian, had much to do with the direction vocation took in Reformed Protestantism. Max Weber's thesis[35] that the Calvinist view of vocation provided the inner motivation for the rise of capitalism has been severely criticized, but the fact remains that this view of vocation, as developed in Puritanism, provided a very convenient rationale for the leaders of the capitalistic enterprise.

In trying to grasp Luther's view of work as an expression of vocation we need to keep in mind (a) when he came on the stage of history and (b) what happened after he left the stage. George Forell helps us to remember both points, at the cost of some oversimplification, by affirming that Rome took the position that "work is an evil, at best a necessary evil," while Geneva took the position that "work is the activity which gives life meaning and zest—it is our purpose in life." According to Rome we work in order to live, but according to Geneva we live in order to work. Luther stands somewhere between these two positions. The solution to the problem of work is not to depreciate it and escape it, if possible, as Roman Catholicism advised; nor is the solution the glorification of work itself as in some way the bearer of salvation, as the Neo-Calvinists seemed to imply. "As Luther saw it, God confronts man *in* his daily work and calls him to responsible discipleship right here." [36]

But Luther himself did not have the whole answer. Some weaknesses in his understanding of vocation have already been implied. In the first place, we must never forget that Luther lived in a predominantly feudal society, and that much of his

[35] *The Protestant Ethic and the Spirit of Capitalism*, trans. by Talcott Parsons (New York: Scribner's, 1930).
[36] George Forell, "Work and the Christian Calling," *The Lutheran Quarterly*, VIII (May, 1956), 105-118.

thought is shaped accordingly. This also explains to a very large extent his social conservatism, his fear of change and his horror of revolution. Secondly, he offers little help to a person struggling with "the choice of a lifework." His consideration of vocation usually proceeded on the assumption that men were already in their life situations or stations. The problem was not how to find "a lifework," but what to do with one's present station. In his writings on education, however, he did urge parents and princes to see to it that young persons of outstanding aptitudes for particular offices would receive the requisite education. In the third place, Luther's eschatology prevented him from taking a long-range view of vocation. Like St. Paul, he had a "foreshortened" view of history. Since he expected the imminent end of the world, he apparently saw no point in working out for either church or culture the far-reaching implications of his concept of vocation.

In addition to admitting these "weaknesses," it is appropriate to express what can be termed "a regret." As noted at the outset of this lecture, Luther clearly affirmed in his Small Catechism and in his Large Catechism the primary biblical meaning of vocation, namely, the calling, gathering, enlightening, and sanctifying of the people of God, the church. It is to be regretted that Luther was forced by historical circumstances to give almost his entire attention to the derivative meaning of vocation, namely, the Christian's life of service, to the neglect of the primary meaning. To have done what he did was, of course, an integral and essential aspect of Luther's own calling. Vocation had to be liberated from the narrow limits imposed by Rome. On the other hand, Luther achieved this liberation at the price of failing to develop fully his doctrine of the church and of placing a severe strain upon the biblical view of vocation.

That his concept of vocation had far-reaching implications no historian has ever denied. After Luther, everyday life was never quite the same again. Partly because he did not bother to

work out the implications, and partly because of the deep sinfulness of human nature (which he well knew!), his concept of
the vocation of the Christian man never realized its potential.
In fact, the perversions of his concept of vocation during the
centuries following Luther down to the present day have been
terrible to behold. Nevertheless, what Luther *did* accomplish
is succinctly summarized in the words of W. R. Forrester:
"Luther, in deposing the monk from his former position as the
ideal of a Christian man, and putting the good householder in
his place, changed the whole emphasis of Christian ethics, and
gave a new start to the history of Europe." [37] In other words,
Luther broke the Roman chains which bound vocation and
extended the calling of God to include the totality of every
Christian's life.

[37] *Christian Vocation*, p. 154.

4

THE CALLING OF EVERYMAN
TODAY

Having explored the meaning of vocation in the Scriptures and in the writings of Martin Luther, it is now time to attempt an answer to the question: What is the calling of Everyman today? The insights gained so far will be utilized in outlining an approach to vocation relevant to our contemporary situation. "Everyman" is taken to mean representative man in the sense of the famous fifteenth-century morality play with that title.

As soon as one mentions "calling" or "vocation" three basic questions come to mind: Who is calling? To whom is the call addressed? For what purpose is the call? They are very simple questions, questions that are implicit or explicit in all kinds of circumstances where a call is heard.

For six years we lived on a certain block of Claremont Avenue in New York City, just across from Columbia University. On the one side of the street stood Barnard College buildings and on the other side of the street stood apartment buildings which housed families of Columbia faculty and staff. Since the street was a dead end, both the street itself and the wide sidewalks became, after school and over week ends, a veritable playground. At those times, above the noise of children at play down below, one could hear, intermittently, a call from the apartments above: "Johnny! Susie!" Who was calling? A mother. To whom was she calling? Her children. For what purpose did she call? To bring them home—for dinner, perhaps, or yet again, to run an errand.

Vocation, understood from the perspective of Christian faith, is as simple as that! Who is calling? God. To whom is the call addressed? His children. For what purpose does he call? That his children may come home, to gather around his Table and then to run errands for him. Let us examine these questions and answers.

The three basic questions

Who is calling? To reply that God is calling may appear to be an obvious answer, at least for Christians, but let's not proceed to the next question too quickly. Consider: In the widespread and casual use of the word "vocation" or "calling," to how many persons does the question of who is calling ever occur?

Pick up the latest and most highly recommended books on vocational guidance which you may see on the library shelves of a school of education or in the office of a high-school counselor and try to find the word "God" in an index. No, you will not find God there because in the professional field which specializes in helping persons "discover" their "vocations" God has long since been banished. And so we have the weird phenomenon today of callings without a caller—no less weird than the smile of the Cheshire cat without the Cheshire cat in *Alice in Wonderland!* Small wonder that a novelist who is a thoroughgoing naturalist can refer without any sense of incongruity to writing as "his calling."

And so the question of who is calling must be raised and answered. It must be raised by Christians on every occasion when the words "calling" and "vocation" are used in a clearly naturalistic sense. By so doing in a sort of socratic way, some persons may be sufficiently annoyed, disturbed, even shocked that they will stop prostituting one of the most significant words in the English language or begin for the first time to wrestle with the fundamental issues of human life and destiny.

But there is another reason for raising the question, namely, to spell out the answer. "God" is indeed the answer, and yet, for the Christian, it is not an adequate answer. Such an answer can be given much too glibly. Furthermore, such a minimal answer may actually turn out to be non-Christian since the concept of God can be given many a different content.

For Christians the One who calls is none other than "God the Father of our Lord Jesus Christ," and this is saying something quite other than "God the unmoved First Mover" and something far more than "the God of Israel." Yes, the answer must be spelled out so that there may be no misunderstanding. Indeed, the answer has been spelled out for us. Why should we struggle with words and phrases when the answer is at hand in the liturgy of the church? He who calls is the one God—Father Almighty, Maker of heaven and of earth, and of all things visible and invisible . . . only-begotten Son, who, for us men, and for our salvation, came down from heaven, and was made man . . . Holy Ghost, the Lord and Giver of life, who proceeds from the Father and the Son, who with the Father and the Son together is worshiped and glorified.

To whom is the call addressed? The call of God is addressed to his children, to all his children, everywhere.

This answer immediately poses the problem of *who* are God's children. According to one view, all human beings are children of God by virtue of being the creatures of God. This view is reflected in the popular concept of "The fatherhood of God and the brotherhood of man," the acceptance of which is supposed to dissolve all difficulties between men and between nations! Those taking this position claim the support of the creation story, which affirms that man was made in God's image (Gen. 1:26-30), and Paul's speech in the Areopagus, to wit: "And [God] made from one every nation of men to live on all the face of the earth, having determined allotted periods and the boundaries of their habitation, that they should seek God, in the hope that they might feel after him and find him. Yet he is not far from each one of us, for 'In him we live and move and have our being'; as even some of your poets have said, 'For we are indeed his offspring' " (Acts 17:26-28). According to the alternative view, both Old and New Testaments have been written in the conviction that men are not children by birth (by creation), but become children of God by adoption. Many passages can be quoted to support this position, as, for example, John 1:12: "To all who received him, who believed in his name, he gave power to become children of God; who were born, not of blood nor of the will of the flesh nor of the will of man, but of God." (Cf. also John 8:44, and Rom. 8 and 9.)

Involved are the unfathomable and endlessly debated issues of election and predestination. For our purpose it can simply be reiterated that God calls his children, and the problem of ultimate identification can then be left in his hands. Perhaps it can be put this way: God calls all men (Acts 17:30) but only his children know his voice and respond to his call (John 10:1-5). This seems to have been Peter's understanding when he addressed that motley crowd on the Day of Pentecost: "The promise is to you and to your children and to all that are far off, every one whom the Lord our God calls to him" (Acts 2:39).

Some of God's children are indeed far off, and others are near; some are rich, and others are poor; some are well educated, and others are illiterate; some sweat it out in coal mines, and others analyze charts of production in air-conditioned offices; some tend assembly lines, and others tend babies; some are married, and others are single; some are old, and others are young— and yet they are all called with the same call. It is the call to Everyman!

For what purpose does God call? God calls his children to come home (Luke 15:11-32), to be faithful members of his household (Eph. 2:19-22), to serve him in the orders of his creation (John 17:15-19).

In other words, God calls Everyman out of his isolation, alienation, and loneliness into fellowship, into a unique fellowship: "God is faithful, by whom you were called into the fellowship [*koinonia*] of his Son, Jesus Christ our Lord" (I Cor. 1:9). For this is a fellowship both human and divine: "We have fellowship with one another, and the blood of Jesus his Son cleanses us from all sin" (I John 1:7). The price of admission into this fellowship is forgiveness, and the price has been paid. Only he who constantly lives in forgiveness is at home in the household of God. And the fellowship of forgiveness is known supremely in the breaking of bread together at the family meal, around the Table of the Lord.

To refer to the fellowship of forgiveness as the household of God is, of course, to use a metaphor to indicate a reality which can never be adequately expressed. Certainly no single metaphor is sufficient in itself to convey the total meaning of the church. Especially illuminating are the metaphors of "the body of Christ" and "the people of God," the former stressing the organic character of the church and the latter the prototype of the church in the people of Israel. Both metaphors emphasize the corporate nature of God's call to Everyman. Christians are "members one of another," be it in a household, a body, or a people.

God calls men, then, to be with him and to be with each other in his household. This is the basic purpose of the divine call, and in a sense it is an "end in itself." But there are errands to be run, functions to be fulfilled, tasks to be done by the various members of the family. To be a member of the household is to have an assignment; both membership and assignment are the gifts of God. Such assignments vary according to (a) the qualifications of the members and (b) their willingness to be of use to the Head of the household.

When God calls Everyman into his family, *ipso facto*, he calls Everyman into the divine service. Everyman's vocation is of one piece, cut from whole cloth. It is a seamless robe, and Everyman will attempt to rend it at his peril. Integral to Everyman's vocation, however, are *two* fields of service—within the household and outside the household—and these fields intersect each other.

This division is made for the purpose of analysis only. In reality we are dealing with the same persons, and with the totality of their lives. The division simply recognizes the fact that these persons, these Christians, are "in the world but not of it," that their "citizenship is in heaven" but presently their lot is cast in "the kingdoms of this world."

Vocation within the household

Let it be clear that under this category we shall not be dealing further with the saving action of God by which Everyman is incorporated into his household. We shall be dealing only with the responsibility of Everyman who is already within the community of the called. This responsibility is threefold: to lead a life worthy of the calling, to minister to the saints, and to declare the wonderful deeds of God.

1. *Every Christian is called "to lead a life worthy of the calling to which [he has] been called,* with all lowliness and meekness, with patience, forbearing one another in love, eager to maintain the unity of the Spirit in the bond of peace" (Eph. 4:1-3).

This familiar passage is illustrative of the extended treatment in the New Testament letters of vocation within the household of faith. It is inconceivable to Paul that members of the body of Christ should lie to one another, steal from one another, slander one another, be covetous of one another, and practice immorality with one another (cf. Col. 3). On the contrary, within the family all believers should "through love be servants of one another" (Gal. 5:13). Members of a family should be so closely bound together in love that "if one member suffers, all suffer together; if one member is honored, all rejoice together" (I Cor. 12:26).

The profusion of Pauline teaching on this subject, however, should not make us unmindful of the rich resources in other parts of the New Testament. For example, the First Letter of John could with much justification be given the title of "A Handbook on Vocation within the Household of Faith." The author does not use the term "vocation" or "calling," but his concern throughout is that the "little children," the members of the family of Christ, should be worthy of the calling to which they have been called. Here is the classic passage (4:7-11):

Beloved, let us love one another; for love is of God, and he who loves is born of God and knows God. He who does not love does not know God; for God is love. In this the love of God was made manifest among us, that God sent his only Son into the world, so that we might live through him. In this is love, not that we loved God but that he loved us and sent his Son to be the expiation for our sins. Beloved, if God so loved us, we also ought to love one another.

The motivation for love within the fellowship of believers has never been set forth more clearly. That which is at the heart of the biblical concept of vocation, namely, the divine initiative, is exalted in this passage as the fountainhead of Christian fellowship.

There have been times and places in the history of the church when outsiders could point to the family of Christ and say, "How these Christians love one another!" But the record of strife within the visible household of faith is so extensive that it literally fills libraries—both the petty strife of personal animosities and the bitter theological strife leading to schism. The disastrous effects of this strife have been as deep as the ocean, and as broad as the sea. Whatever else may be said about these effects, this can be affirmed: strife within the household of faith is a denial of Christian vocation. For the life we are called to live within the household is one of lowliness, meekness, patience, forbearing love, eagerness to maintain the unity of the Spirit in the bond of peace.

2. *Every Christian is called to minister to the saints.* The

primary New Testament word for ministry is *diakonia*, the meaning of which is "service." Translators differ as to how it should be rendered in the many contexts in which it appears. For example, Hebrews 6:10 can with equal justification be translated either "to minister to the saints" or "to be of service to the saints." Postponing until later consideration of an ordained ministry, it is perfectly clear in the New Testament that all members of the household of God are expected to minister to the saints, i.e., to each other. This responsibility can be exercised in several ways.

Each member of the family is called to minister to the *physical needs* of his brothers in Christ. A Christian can to some extent carry out a ministry to physical needs in face-to-face relationships. Within his own congregation there are always opportunities to minister to those closest to him: a child who has fallen needs to be picked up; a woman needs help in the nursing of her aged father; a fellow-student needs tutorial assistance to master a difficult subject; a hospitalized member needs to be visited. But beyond the immediate reach of his own hand a Christian can greatly extend his ministry by giving financially to the physical relief and rehabilitation programs of his church. This stewardship of material resources thereby becomes a part of his vocation.

Christians are also called to minister to each other's *spiritual needs*. And so Paul writes to the Colossians (3:16): "Let the word of Christ dwell in you richly, as you teach and admonish one another in all wisdom." Wisdom in spiritual matters is not the exclusive possession of the ordained pastor; neither is the responsibility for teaching and admonishing the members of the household of faith vested only in the professional clergy! To the Galatians Paul writes: "Brethren, if a man is overtaken in any trespass, you who are spiritual should restore him in a spirit of gentleness" (6:1). Here is a difficult ministry to spiritual needs which, says Paul, can properly be carried out by any member of the household who is sufficiently "spiritual."

All Christians, then, have a ministry to each other, a ministry

to physical and spiritual needs. This is an integral part of their
vocations. Most Christians carry out such a ministry quietly
within the limits of their aptitudes; but some Christians receive
special gifts which bring their ministry special recognition. And
so Paul writes to the Corinthians (I Cor. 12) that "there are
varieties of gifts, but the same Spirit; and there are varieties of
service [ministry], but the same Lord"; and proceeds to list
eleven specially identified services rendered in the church. These
services should not be performed with a view to honor but rather
in such a fashion that all members of the body of Christ "may
have the same care for one another." (Special functions and
offices in the church will be considered in the next lecture.)

3. *Every Christian is called to declare the wonderful deeds of
God.* Addressing the church, the author of I Peter (2:9-10) asks
in effect: Why do you think God has "called you out of darkness into his marvelous light," and has designated you as "a
chosen race, a royal priesthood, a holy nation, God's own people"? Answer: "that you may declare the wonderful deeds of
him who called you" to those that are still in darkness.

This part of Everyman's vocation in the church merges almost
imperceptibly with his vocation in the world. Indeed, it is the
point at which the church moves into the world to fulfil her
mission there in response to her Lord's command, "You shall be
my witnesses in Jerusalem and in all Judea and Samaria and to
the end of the earth" (Acts 1:8).

Everyman's vocation within the household of faith is to support the church with his prayers and his gifts as the church
undertakes to carry out her mission of witness in areas where
Everyman himself cannot declare the wonderful deeds of God.
He can make his witness in his own station in the world, in the
place where he is, but Everyman himself cannot directly witness
to Christ "to the end of the earth." And so his vocation, it again
appears, includes the stewardship of his material resources.

The Spirit of God calls his children by means of the church, to which has been entrusted his Word. On the one hand, there is the *life* of the church, the life within the household nourished by Word and sacrament; on the other hand, there is the *mission* of the church, which flows from her life into the world. The strength of the church's mission depends upon the vitality of life within the household of faith; and, in turn, the vitality of life within the household depends in no small measure upon the church's acceptance of her mission outside the household.

The mission of the church is a corporate mission. This is said at the risk of redundancy because the calling of Everyman to declare the wonderful deeds of God must be seen within this corporate mission. As we have noted, this truth becomes obvious when the gifts of one Christian must be joined with the gifts of many other Christians in order to plant the church in some remote corner of the earth. Everyman must also recognize this truth as he attempts to declare the deeds of God in his own community, in the office, in the factory, in the classroom; for even there he does not make his witness alone or in his own strength. As he seeks to fulfil this aspect of his vocation he must do so as a member of the body of Christ, within the fellowship of a royal priesthood, undergirded by the prayers of the whole household of God. For Everyman to try to witness to Christ "on his own" is to court frustration and defeat, for his calling to make Christ known is set within the mission of the whole church.

To summarize: Everyman's vocation within the household of faith is to walk worthily of the calling to which he has been called, to minister according to his gifts to the physical and spiritual needs of the saints, and to declare either directly or indirectly the wonderful deeds of God.

Vocation outside the household

Everyman is called to live both in the church and in the world.

A Christian always wrestles with a double temptation: either to identify himself completely with the world, and thereby lose his soul, or to escape from the world, and thereby disclaim human needs and the divine command. The call of God does not take Everyman out of the world but places him squarely in the world. A Christian knows, of course, that unless he is constantly being transformed by the renewing of his mind through life in the household of faith he will inevitably be conformed to the world and fail to fulfil his vocation there.

At the outset let it be bluntly affirmed that according to our Christian understanding *no man has a vocation in the world unless he has a vocation in the church.* John Smith may have an excellent job, for which he is highly qualified and to which he is completely dedicated, but if God has not called him into the household of faith John Smith has no vocation. Let it be said with equal bluntness that *vocation cannot be equated with occupation, although vocation may include occupation.* In contrast to any delimitation let it be affirmed once again that a Christian's vocation includes every facet of his life.

Here is Hans Mueller, a mechanic. It so happens that Hans is the son of an immigrant couple, still living; he has recently become a citizen of the United States; he is a member of the local labor union; he is a registered Democrat; he and his wife have been married twelve years, and they have two children; his house is so located that he has three close neighbors; and he is a member of St. Paul's Church on Kensington Avenue. Is Hans's vocation being a mechanic? Not at all! God calls Hans into the household of faith and into his service to be a competent mechanic, a devoted son, a loyal citizen, a responsible member of his labor union and his political party, a faithful husband, a wise father, and a good neighbor. His vocation includes all these established relationships as well as all the casual relationships that vary from day to day.

In all these relationships Everyman is called to glorify God.

If "the heavens are telling the glory of God" (Ps. 19:1), certainly Everyman should "ascribe to the Lord the glory due his name" (Ps. 96:8). And this is accomplished not only by bringing an offering and coming into his courts "to worship the Lord in holy array," but by doing everything to the glory of God (I Cor. 10:31).

What does the glorification of God mean, then, in terms of Everyman's vocation outside the household of faith?

1. *A Christian's vocation is to glorify God by being of service to all men regardless of their status.* A Christian is called not only to minister to those of the household of faith but also to serve all men—Jew and Gentile, black and white, American and non-American. Everyman's vocation in the world is to translate the law of love (Luke 10:27) into "specifics."

In this regard Everyman's vocation is shaped by the need of his neighbor. And this includes the total need of the neighbor. An escaped victim of totalitarian terrorism needs to have his wounds cared for, but the matter does not end there. Having lost all his material resources, he needs food and shelter, but the matter does not end there. After he has recovered his health he needs work to do if he is to maintain his self-respect and meet his obligations in society, but the matter does not end there. Even though he is meeting his obligations to society (after a fashion, perhaps!), he still needs to come to terms with his Creator, and to know the peace which passes all understanding. Everyman's vocation is to help his neighbor meet all these needs, and this involves the whole range of service from social welfare to evangelism. In the words of Paul as addressed to the Corinthians, "under the test of this service, you will glorify God by your obedience in acknowledging the gospel of Christ, and by the generosity of your contribution for them [the saints] *and for all others*" (II Cor. 9:13).

Everyman is called to serve his neighbor not only through his monetary contributions and through his personal action on behalf of his neighbor's welfare; he is also called by God to serve his neighbor by acting responsibly toward the structures of society. In other words, service to all men involves not only social welfare but also social justice. His vocation lays upon him, for example, a responsibility both for the victims of totalitarianism and for totalitarianism itself. "This means," in the words of Joseph Sittler, "that the will to help must devise the means to help in ways determined by the actual collectivities within which men are deepeningly involved, and within which interdependency relates each man to all men by a thousand cords. Needs that are shaped by structures must be met by help that also is structured." [1] Everyman is called to work for justice, because "justice is a primary instrument of love and a field for its operations." [2]

The relationship of social welfare and social justice within Christian vocation is clearly and succinctly expressed in several of the theses of the Third Assembly of the Lutheran World Federation, as, for example, theses four and five of Section IV:

Thus we are called to translate love and compassion into the structures of justice. In matters of civil liberties and racial integration, of concern for the uprooted and for people in areas of rapid social change, and of care for the mentally and physically disabled, our love fails if it does not materialize in recognition of human rights.

Where justice falls short in the complexities and the brokenness of our human endeavors, there especially the Christian finds his calling to follow his Lord in service and suffering. Freed by Christ and quickened by the Holy Spirit, he exercises the inventiveness of love.[3]

At this point something must be said about Everyman's responsibility for his own physical and mental well-being. Three perversions must be identified and rejected. *First,* there is the

---

[1] Harold C. Letts (ed.), *Life in Community* (*Christian Social Responsibility* III) (Philadelphia: Muhlenberg Pr., 1957), p. 30.

[2] *Ibid.,* p. 32.

[3] *Messages of the Third World Assembly,* Section IV, theses 1-5 (Minneapolis: Augsburg, 1957), pp. 113-14.

view that since we are saved by grace, and only the soul is of importance anyhow, what we do with our bodies is of no great consequence. *Secondly*, there is the view of the medieval church that bodily discipline is an instrument of salvation: to fast, to scourge oneself, to wear uncomfortable clothes, and to sleep in even more uncomfortable beds accrued to the Christian's celestial credit. *Thirdly*, there is the view of the physical culturists and the intellectual purists that a perfect figure and a razor-sharp mind are their own justification, i.e., figure for figure's sake and mind for mind's sake. Over against these perversions stands the biblical view: in his vocation Everyman will care for his body and mind as a craftsman cares for his tools.

2. *A Christian's vocation is to glorify God by making the best possible use of the gifts God has given him.* This is applicable, of course, to the use of gifts within as well as outside the household of faith. Everyman should use his special endowments in both realms. In fact, to draw the line between the sacred and the secular is frequently very difficult.

John Sebastian Bach wrote all his music *sub specie aeternitatis*. He did not compose to please his benefactors, or to win the plaudits of an audience or of a congregation. At the top of each score he put two sets of initials: SDG—*Soli Deo Gloria*, to the glory of God alone, and JJ—*Jesu Juva*, help me, Jesus. As Albert Schweitzer points out in his great work on Bach, these initials were to him no mere formulas. "Music is an act of worship with Bach. His artistic activity and his personality are both based on his faith. . . . All great art, even secular, is in itself religious in his eyes; for him the tones do not perish, but ascend to God like praise too deep for utterance." In Bach's own words, music "should have no other end and aim than the glory of God and the re-creation of the soul; where this is not kept in mind there is no true music, but only an infernal clamour and ranting." [4]

⁴ Albert Schweitzer, *J. S. Bach*, trans. by Ernest Newman (London: Black, 1911), I, 166-67.

Bach is an excellent example of a Christian who in his vocation uses his gifts to the glory of God both in the church and in the world. Whether one is listening to the *St. Matthew's Passion* or to the *Brandenburg Concertos* the music seems to "ascend to God like praise too deep for utterance." One senses unmistakably the dimensions of depth and height; one becomes aware of a frame of reference whose parapets are in eternity.

Well, someone may be thinking, that's true enough for Bach, but what about more ordinary mortals? What about Christians whose gifts are in fields such as construction, industry, farming, medicine, government, the fine arts, teaching? How can these persons use their aptitudes, their skills to the glory of God? This is perhaps the most difficult question in any consideration of vocation in the workaday world. There are no easy answers: in fact, at many points there are no answers—at least not yet. Some things are clear, however, and need to be said.

For one thing, Christians engaged in construction, industry, farming, medicine, government, the fine arts, teaching are *called to glorify God in and through these fields* and not merely in peripheral ways, that is, in ways which have no necessary connection with the fields themselves. Take teaching. Here is a Christian who is a professor of sociology. Note that I did not refer to him as a "Christian teacher." This would have been a misnomer because he has neatly divided his life into two compartments. As a Christian he feels that he is discharging his responsibilities by ushering once a month at First Church, by serving as adviser to the campus religious council, and by being available to his students for counseling. When he enters the classroom, however, he leaves his Christian faith behind and becomes a naturalist! A Christian whose lifework is teaching cannot fulfil his vocation unless he glorifies God in and through his teaching. To glorify God his scholarship must, of course, be sound and his pedagogy effective; but, beyond that, his teaching must be within a discernible Christian frame of reference.

A second thing that needs to be said about a Christian's making the best possible use of the gifts God has given him is this: *piety is no substitute for competence.* The point has already been implied but it must be made explicit. It is not enough that a Christian engineer be "sincere," a faithful member of St. John's Church by the town hall, and a leader of family worship in his home. A Christian engineer will not glorify God unless he is technically proficient. All the prayers of himself, his family, and St. John's congregation cannot be counted on to save the suspension bridge he designed from collapsing into the river if he has not provided adequately for the stresses and strains of a one-hundred-mile-per-hour wind! Not to be competent is both an affront to the Creator who endowed him with gifts and a callous betrayal of his neighbors whom he is called to serve in love.

Closely related to the question of competence is the matter of *integrity*, especially in the arts and crafts. God's creative gifts can be used to his glory only if the work of artists and craftsmen reveals an essential honesty, an inner truthfulness. God desires "truth in the inward being," as the psalmist says (51:6), and without this truth in the arts and crafts God is not being glorified. The creative gifts bestowed by God are so easily and so frequently prostituted to ignoble ends. When artists and craftsmen create what the public wants rather than what they know is sound; when they use their gifts to produce what will sell rather than what is honest; when they yield to pressures for that which is cheap, artificial, and hollow—then is integrity forfeited, and the Christian who yields to such temptations has to that extent failed in his vocation.

3. *A Christian's vocation to glorify God must be grounded in God's command and renewed by his grace.* To put it another way, only by divine command and by divine grace can a Christian have a vocation in the world. Here we are deeply indebted to Luther for establishing the only basis upon which Everyman

can be in the world and not of it. Let us recall his concept of the two realms (cf. pp. 50-51).

A Christian lives in two realms, in two dimensions—the dimension of grace and the dimension of law. In the *realm of grace* Everyman is given the pure righteousness of Christ and the unqualified freedom of the sons of God. This is the realm of absolutes, the dimension of perfection. Here the only compulsion is the constraint of the love of Christ. In the *realm of law* only "civil" righteousness can be realized, and Everyman's freedoms are severely limited. This is the realm of relativities, of compromise, of rough justice. Without external compulsion anarchy would prevail. Both realms belong to God, and to both the forgiven sinner belongs.

As Everyman seeks to fulfil his vocation outside the household of faith he must remember that he really is in the world. He must accept his place in the orders of creation and be subject to the compulsions of these orders. What is more, as Everyman seeks to serve his fellows in the structures of these orders he will be required to effect compromises (viewed in the light of absolutes) that greater evil may not prevail.

Therefore, it is affirmed that Everyman can play his role in society, and especially in the political and economic orders, only because of the command of God and the grace of God. On the one hand, it is God's will that the orders of creation be maintained, and that Everyman accept his proper share of responsibility to uphold these orders. On the other hand, when Everyman in government or in industry commits evil that greater evil may not prevail the evil done is still evil, and must be forgiven if Everyman is to live also in thé realm of grace. The forgiveness of God not only cleanses the hands of his servants doing his work in the world; it also "lets loose" in the world through these servants fresh streams of renewal and creativity.

One of the great contributions which Gustaf Wingren has made to our understanding of Christian vocation is at this point.

Although he demonstrates in a masterful way the necessity of distinguishing between the two realms, he writes as follows:

Love born of faith and the Spirit effects a complete breakthrough of the boundary between the two kingdoms, the wall of partition between heaven and earth, as did God's incarnation in Christ. . . . Faith transfers to love the freedom from law it had in heaven, so that love on earth carries with it faith's own freedom from law. . . . God descends from heaven and transforms the earth, now here, now there, as faith and love appear through the church's preaching of the gospel, through the spiritual realm. The task of the church includes a continuing renewal of the worldly orders, a never-ending alertness in all vocations, from the princely to the meanest labor.[5]

Everyman's exercise of his vocation is so much of the time pedestrian, motivated by obligation and mellowed by the divine consolation; but when the flame of faith burns brightly and the Spirit breaks through the crust of routine experience then his vocation takes wings and each moment is transfigured with joy.

To summarize: Everyman's vocation outside the household of faith gives him as his perennial task the glorification of God in every facet of his life. It summons him to glorify God through loving service to all men; it challenges him to make the most fruitful use of the gifts God has given him; and it equips him by divine command and grace to be effectively instrumental to God in the realization of his purposes for the whole creation.

Living in vocation

We come finally to the questions: How can Everyman live in his vocation? How can his vocation come alive for him? How can his call from God lay hold upon Everyman in such a compelling way that his whole existence is transformed? Here are five simple but basic suggestions addressed not to the unbeliever

[5] Wingren, *op. cit.*, pp. 46-48.

but to *Everyman who is already a member of the household of faith and yet for whom vocation is unreal*. They are addressed to him who can honestly confess: "the Holy Ghost has called me by the Gospel . . . even as He calls, gathers, enlightens, and sanctifies the whole Church." And they are addressed to Everyman personally.

1. *Be a faithful member of the household of God.*

Here your vocation began, and this is where it must take roots and grow. The sense of vocation is strong in proportion to the strength of faith, and faith is fed by Word and sacrament. Without the Word of forgiveness and the sacramental fellowship in the family of Christ faith will wither like a plant deprived of water, and the sense of vocation will grow dim. Living vocation means constancy in the hearing of the Word and in the reception of the Sacrament of the Lord's Supper.

It also means accepting your responsibilities within the household of God—to love and honor members of the family of Christ, to minister as you can to their several needs, and to share with them the mission of the church to make Christ known to the end of the earth. As you fulfil this part of your vocation within the household of faith, you may expect to see your vocation outside the household of faith take on meaning and power.

2. *Respond in obedience to the claims God makes upon your life.*

You know very well some of the claims God is making upon your life at this moment. Respond in obedience! God's call will be heard in more and more of your activities and relationships as you respond in obedience to those claims which are now unmistakably clear. If you are obedient in one task God will call you to another task, and as you are obedient in many tasks assurance of vocation will grow. But how does God reveal his will for each member of his household? How does he make his claims known?

Einar Billing would reply that God reveals His will in the

forgiveness of sins. "It is worthy of note," he says, "that the forgiveness of sins gives not only the motive and power to accomplish a deed already planned, but it gives first of all the deed itself, that is, clarity as to what deed God desires of me." [6] Gustaf Wingren would reply that God makes his claims known in the context of persons and events in which we live. This is the way he puts it: "God does not come to man in thoughts and feelings which well up in him when he isolates himself from the world, but rather in what happens to man in the external and tangible events which take place about him." [7] Whether God lays his claims upon you through the forgiveness of sin or through people and events (and he does both!), obedience is a condition of your continuing to hear his voice.

3. *Rejoice in your present station in life but don't accept it as final.*

Although your station in life may be far from ideal, be grateful that you do have a place in God's world and that he has given you neighbors to serve. On the other hand, never regard your station in life as final. Christians live in a dynamic world, and serve a creative God. Just as we are pilgrims on earth, so we are pilgrims in our stations in life. Some stations are more stable than others but the stability of no station is absolutely assured. The phenomenon of physical mobility in America gives new meaning to the ancient word, "Here we have no lasting city" (Heb. 13:14)! As the world's needs change, and as your qualifications change (for better or for worse), the shape of your vocation in the world is subject to change. What God wills for you today may not be what he wills for you tomorrow.

Therefore, both acceptance and openness are necessary if your vocation is to remain alive. You must accept your present station and, so far as possible, live in it to the glory of God; at the same

---

[6] *Our Calling,* trans. by Conrad Bergendoff (Rock Island: Augustana, 1951), p. 24.

[7] Wingren, *op. cit.,* p. 117.

time, you must be open to the call of God to serve him in new ways or in different circumstances. Part of this openness is constant willingness to prepare yourself for service more fully commensurate with your God-given talents. If you are now a student remember that preparation in itself is just as much vocation under God as being the physician you hope someday to be. Stations may change, but vocation is continuous. A Christian may leave his station but he cannot leave his vocation—and still be Christian!

4. *Grow in your knowledge of yourself and of the various fields of your vocation.*

God gave you your vocation but he did not give you (by revelation!) the factual knowledge necessary to translate your calling into effective action both within the household of faith and outside the household. In all the roles you are called upon to play—be it that of engineer or of brother or of husband or of citizen—you are under obligation to equip yourself to play the roles well. Failure to do so may very well result in a state of confusion and uncertainty regarding your calling. Growth in knowledge about the various fields of your vocation should always be accompanied by a comparable growth in knowledge about yourself. If your understanding of yourself is superficial or inaccurate, your whole vocation can take on a semblance of unreality.

This mandate applies also to the young man or woman wrestling with the problem of what his or her lifework ought to be. To participation in the community of believers, obedience to the divine commands, and gratitude for opportunities of immediate service should be added careful evaluation of personal aptitudes and of human needs. Testing, consultation with experts, and study of possible fields of labor all have their proper places in the unfolding of divine will for a person standing on the threshold of life. No Christian will ever regard these techniques as being autonomous, as alone constituting sufficient guidance, but they can be used by God to help reveal his purposes. To neglect them would be as irresponsible as the attempt of a surgeon to perform a difficult operation without making use of the best available instruments.

5. Pray for God's guidance and help in every aspect of your vocation.

Prayer is, of course, no substitute for obedience to divine commands. If you are not responding daily to the unmistakable claims God is making upon your life the feeling of unreality about your vocation will not be remedied simply by praying. On the other hand, obedience divorced from prayer degenerates into mere legalism, and legalism is just about as deadly as disobedience. The common temptation of the Christian is to make his decisions and to attempt to carry out his plans without bothering to consult the King of creation either because of sheer indifference and lack of faith or because he is consciously or unconsciously evading God, whose commands he would rather not hear.

If you believe that God is, that he cares, that you are a member of his own household by virtue of his personal call, then how ridiculous it is that you should hesitate to speak with him frankly about your vocation. "Ask, and it will be given you; seek, and you will find; knock, and it will be opened to you. For every one who asks receives, and he who seeks finds, and to him who knocks it will be opened" (Luke 11:9-10). This is the promise of your Lord!

Living in vocation, then, is living in the household of God, the family of Christ, the Holy Catholic Church; it is living in obedience to God in all things, both great and small; it is living in gratitude for what God has given and in openness for whatever he has in store; it is living in commitment to grow in understanding of self and of one's fields of service; it is living in the posture of prayer so that God may always have free access to the innermost soul. So to live is to know with exceeding great joy the vocation God has in store for Everyman.

5

PROFESSIONAL SERVICE IN THE CHURCH

God the Father of our Lord Jesus Christ calls his children into the household of faith and to loving service both in the church and in the world. This is the vocation of Everyman. It is one vocation, but God does not call "once for all"; rather, he calls and continues to call through his Spirit as Everyman responds in faith and obedience.

Now we come to a fork in the road at the point of remunerative employment. A very important part of the vocation of every Christian is the service for which he receives financial compensation. Most Christians are employed by so-called secular organizations—manufacturing companies, banking institutions, government agencies, schools and colleges, etc. A few Christians are employed by the churches. On the one hand are the millions whose occupations are labeled "secular," and on the other hand are the thousands whose occupations are labeled "ecclesiastical."

Of what significance is this fork in the road in terms of Christian vocation? Is ecclesiastical employment to be preferred to secular employment? Are ecclesiastical occupations on a higher plane than secular occupations? If so, in what sense are they "higher"? If not, why do we so often refer to the holy ministry but never to the holy steel industry? Is a call to the lifework in the church qualitatively different from a call to a lifework in industry, in agriculture, or in education?

Popular as well as quasi-technical parlance seems to indicate that there is a significant difference. The clergy is sharply distinguished from the laity, despite the fact that in the Bible *laos* includes all of the people of God. In fact, the term "layman" has been so degraded by usage that it now means a person who lacks any competence in a given field, a layman's knowledge being contrasted to that of the expert.

For many, many decades (and still to a considerable extent even today) those employed by the churches have been referred to as giving "full-time Christian service." Thousands upon thousands of passionate appeals have been made to youth to eschew worldly occupations and to go into full-time Christian service. It is amazing how supposedly intelligent and biblically oriented persons can make such appeals in blatant disregard of the fact, that, according to the Scriptures, *every Christian is called to serve God on a full-time basis.* When Paul made his appeal to the Christians in Rome "to present your bodies as a living sacrifice, holy and acceptable to God" (12:1), he was certainly not talking about a part-time arrangement.

To a very large extent the phrase "full-time Christian service" has now been replaced by an almost equally misleading label, namely, "church vocations." Every major Protestant denomination uses the label for church work which is financially compensated, either on a salary or on a subsistence basis. John Oliver Nelson has included forty-eight such positions in his "Listing of Church Vocations," [1] and the list includes positions as diversified as pastor, office secretary, sexton, expert in radio, houseparent, and relief worker. Apparently, the criterion applied in most instances for admission to the listing was not "what the work is" but "for whom the work is being done." In other words, there seems to be nothing intrinsically different about "church vocations," except the ministry of Word and sacrament; broadly interpreted, they are merely extrinsically different because a church, rather than a business firm, pays the salaries.

[1] Published by the National Council of Churches of Christ in the U.S.A.

The objection to this label, however, goes much deeper than this. When "church vocations" is applied to those occupations for which remuneration is paid by the churches, the implication is that all other occupations are not church vocations, i.e., have no essential relation to the church, its life, or its concerns. And such a divorcement is doubtless quite in order in the case of certain occupations, e.g., dope-peddling, safe-cracking, and car-stealing! *But the occupation of every Christian is church vocation in the sense that his vocation comes to life in the church, remains rooted in the church, and is nourished by the church.* To say that a church office secretary has a church vocation and to deny that characterization to the consecrated service of a Christian nurse in a city hospital makes no sense whatsoever. Furthermore, the use of the label "church vocations" tends to perpetuate the error that vocation is a synonym for occupation.

Therefore, having discarded "full-time Christian service" and "church vocations" as adequate descriptive labels for ecclesiastical occupations, I have entitled this lecture "Professional Service in the Church." The rationale for this selection will, I hope, become clear as the lecture proceeds.

The ministry in the New Testament

The ministry in the New Testament is, of course, a very extensive, technical and generally abstruse subject. Over the centuries the most brilliant scholars have been unable to settle the issues and the most illustrious church councils have been unable to resolve the differences of interpretation. My aim here is simply to state a point of view.

As already noted in the fourth lecture, the primary New Testament word for ministry is *diakonia*, the literal meaning of which is "service" (in classical Greek the serving of food or drink). Translators differ as to how it should be rendered in the various contexts. For example, the King James Version translates

Matthew 20:28 as follows: "The Son of man came not to be ministered unto but to minister." The Revised Standard Version, however, reads as follows: "The Son of man came not to be served but to serve." The Greek words in question are passive and active forms, respectively, of the verb *diakonein*, to serve. It is both a technical and a subjective matter to decide when *diakonia* should be translated "ministry" and when "service."

Another New Testament word for ministry is *leitourgia*, which in classical Greek means a service rendered to the state, usually at a person's own expense. In the Revised Standard Version *leitourgia* (and its related forms) are variously translated as "ministry," "service," "worship," "sacrifice," etc. For example, Hebrews 8:6 is rendered as follows: "Christ has obtained a ministry [*leitourgias*] which is as much more excellent than the old as the covenant he mediates is better, since it is enacted on better promises" (cf. Rom. 15:16 or Phil. 2:25). On the other hand, II Corinthians 9:12 is translated, "For the rendering of this service [*leitourgias*] not only supplies the wants of the saints but also overflows in many thanksgivings to God" (cf. Luke 1:23 or Phil. 2:30). Again, determination of meaning in each instance is both a technical and a subjective matter.

An examination of the uses of *diakonia* and *leitourgia* must be supplemented, of course, by a comprehensive study of the church in the New Testament before an understanding can be reached as to the nature of the ministry in the New Testament. Such an approach, I believe, leads to the following conclusions:

1. *The ministry is a general, rather than a restrictive, concept and includes a variety of services.*

In the fourth chapter of the letter to the Ephesians the unity of the church is stressed in terms of its being "one body and one Spirit" and having "one Lord, one faith, one baptism," and then the letter goes on to say that "grace was given to each of us according to the measure of Christ's gift. . . . And his gifts were that some should be apostles, some prophets, some evangelists, some pastors and teachers, *for the equipment of the saints, for the work of ministry, for building up the body of Christ,* until we all attain to the unity of the faith and of the knowledge of the Son of God, to mature manhood, to the measure of the stature of the fulness of Christ" (4:7, 11-13. Italics mine). It is important to note that in this passage "the work of ministry" appears to be synonymous with "the equipment of the saints" and "building up the body of Christ"—also descriptive phrases of a general nature. Apostles, prophets, evangelists, pastors, and teachers all share in this ministry; no one category of service can claim the ministry for its own.

This understanding receives extended support in the well-known twelfth chapter of First Corinthians where Paul affirms that "there are varieties of service" (*diakonion*), which can be just as well translated "there are varieties of ministry" (12:4). He then proceeds to list eleven different "workings" in the body of Christ, including not only prophecy and teaching but also performing miracles, healing, speaking in tongues, and simply helping!

These passages in Ephesians and First Corinthians are further corroborated in the twelfth chapter of Romans (especially vss. 4-8). Paul describes Christians as members of the body of Christ, each member having a different function according to the gifts of the Spirit. It is significant that his illustrative list of functions includes not only prophecy, teaching, and exhortation but also contributing funds, giving aid, and doing acts of mercy.

2. *The ministry, being of a general and inclusive nature, belongs to the body of Christ as a whole.*

The ministry is not the exclusive prerogative of the apostles, even though the apostles are the members of the household of faith who are held in the highest regard. Jesus himself chose the twelve, but the twelve do not lay exclusive claim to the ministry. Neither is it affirmed in the later New Testament writings that the ministry is entirely in the hands of elders or of bishops.

This is true because no one member of the household of faith, and no small coterie of members, possesses all the gifts of the Spirit. These gifts are distributed among many different members, from the lowliest to the highest, each member performing a function for which he is peculiarly qualified. This is not to say that several functions cannot occasionally be performed by one person, as was certainly the case in the primitive church and has been the case in succeeding centuries.

Not only does the ministry belong to the whole body of Christ; the whole body of Christ bears responsibility for the ministry, so that "all things should be done decently and in order" (I Cor. 14:40). Without order the rich and diverse manifestations of the Spirit result in chaos in the household of God.

3. *The ministry of the church is a ministry which its members can bring to each other.*

Within the household of faith there is a mutual ministry, as already noted in the fourth lecture. This ministry can take place in the public assemblies of the believers, where different members make contributions according to their gifts. This ministry can also be exercised outside the assemblies in personal relationships between believers.

This mutual ministry is directed to both physical and spiritual needs, as we have seen. Gifts are sent not only to congregations in need but also to individuals, such as Paul in prison. And within each congregation members certainly ministered to each other's physical needs. A mutual ministry was also carried on in terms of spiritual needs, and this involved teaching, admonishing, and restoration to the fellowship of the household.

As Christians minister to each other, especially in the spiritual realm, they are manifesting in one way the priesthood of all believers, a much misunderstood concept. No believer is a priest in isolation from other believers. This teaching of the New Testament cannot be viewed simply as "the right of the individual to approach God directly." The doctrine of the priesthood of all believers is based on five passages (I Pet. 2:4-5; 2:9-10; Rev. 1:5-6; 5:9-10; 20:6), and all five passages refer to the priesthood in a corporate rather than in an individual sense. All members of the household of God together constitute "a holy priesthood," or "a royal priesthood," which they exercise on behalf of Christ, the great and final High Priest. Each believer can exercise a priestly function in relation to his fellow-believers, and believers together as the body of Christ can exercise a priestly function in relation to the world.

4. *Because the ministry belongs to the whole body of Christ, the church can designate certain members to perform special assignments or offices on its behalf.*

Accordingly, the church at a very early stage in its history designated seven members to assume special responsibility for the distribution of food to the believers. Said the twelve: "Pick out from among you seven men of good repute, full of the Spirit and of wisdom, whom we may appoint to this duty." After the whole body of the disciples had made the selection, we read that "these they set before the apostles, and they prayed and laid their hands upon them." (Acts 6:1-6.) Likewise, the Book of Acts relates that "while [the believers] were worshiping the Lord and fasting, the Holy Spirit said, 'Set apart for me Barnabas and Saul for the work to which I have called them.' Then after fasting and praying they laid their hands on them and sent them off." (13:2-3.) It is important to note that the church's responsibility to designate persons for special assignments or offices can be exercised through persons who had already received the church's approbation (cf. Titus 1:5).

Those selected for special assignments or offices were sometimes formally commissioned or ordained by the churches, although the pattern or procedure for such an action is not clear. It is clear that formal ordination was not necessary to validate the special assignments or offices to which reference is made in the New Testament. H. Grady Davis seems to be entirely justified in concluding that "it is impossible to think ordination was an indispensable rite with a fixed meaning in the New Testament Church."[2]

There remains the question as to how these special assignments or offices were determined. I know of no better answer than that given in "The Report of the Commission on the Doctrine of the Ministry," which was adopted "as a guide to the church" by the 1952 convention of The United Lutheran Church in America.

[In the New Testament church] *roles and offices are shaped by institutional, social, cultural processes; the church as an institution produces them; the natural division of labor, the assigning of roles, is beginning here in the early days of the church's institutional life; it is subject to the control of group expediency.*

This is true not only of the deacon's service, but also with respect to preaching. *The function of preaching is indispensable to the church's life* (Rom. 10:14-15). The church cannot exist unless men call on the name of the Lord, they cannot call on Him in whom they have not believed, and they cannot believe in Him of whom they have not heard. *It is absolutely necessary, therefore, that they hear, and they cannot hear without a preacher.* But the forms and occasions of that preaching are variable, as is the personal status of the preacher, and there are many variations in the New Testament. These are subject to circumstance, opportunity, expediency. No form, no official personnel, is indispensable, as is the function.[3]

To summarize: In the New Testament the ministry is a general concept, and includes a variety of services. Consequently, the ministry is the prerogative and responsibility of the whole body of Christ. This responsibility can be exercised by the members of the household of faith in a ministry to each other. The responsibility can also be exercised by action of the household of faith in designating certain persons to perform special assignments or offices on behalf of the whole church.

[2] "The Ministry in the New Testament," *Chicago Lutheran Theological Seminary Record*, LVII, No. 3, 27.
[3] *Minutes, 1952*, p. 546.

The ministry in the church today

In contrast to the New Testament era, today in the church the ministry is a restrictive concept. In the major Protestant denominations the ordained ministry includes only those who are authorized to preach the Word and administer the sacraments in some way. The phrase "in some way" is used advisedly because many in the ordained ministries of the denominations are rather far removed from preaching and the sacraments, at least as traditionally understood.

It is certainly true of the Lutheran churches that the ordained ministry has had its *raison d'etre* only in the preaching of the Word and the administration of the sacraments, which are regarded as the marks of the church. According to the Augsburg Confession, "the office of teaching the Gospel and administering the Sacraments was instituted" that men may come to faith (Article V); "no one should publicly teach in the Church or administer the Sacraments, unless he be regularly called" (Article XIV); and "to those to whom has been committed the ministry of the Word and Sacraments, no jurisdiction belongs, except to forgive sins, to discern doctrine, to reject doctrines contrary to the Gospel, and to exclude from the communion of the Church wicked men, whose wickedness is known, and this without human force, simply by the Word" (Article XXVIII).

Furthermore, the Lutheran churches are very insistent that the ministry of Word and sacrament is an office and not an order. Therefore, ordination confers no indelible powers, and is not necessarily for life. Ordination is the public recognition of the action of the church in granting authority to proclaim the Word and administer the sacraments to a person properly called to perform these functions. Whenever an ordained minister no longer has a call to perform these functions, or when, as a matter of fact, he does not perform these functions, the church body which ordained him normally requests the return of his ordination papers, and removes him from its roster of clergy. Unless such an action is taken for disciplinary reasons, it should not reflect adversely upon the individual.

In what sense, then, is the office of Word and sacrament a "holy calling"? Again, the Commission on the Doctrine of the Ministry offers wise counsel.

The Ministry is not to be unduly exalted above other callings. All callings which, in the order of creation, contribute to community are equally holy. It is not, therefore, a degradation or a sign of unfaithfulness, if a man leaves the ministry for another calling. What is decisive, and what may be disgraceful, is his reason for doing so. But equally disgraceful may be his reason for coveting the prerogatives of the ministry (cf. Simon Magus). In either case a man must feel himself called of God to that specific function.

On the other hand, *the ministry is not to be degraded and made common.* The office of Word and Sacrament not only lends dignity and authority, but also makes exacting demands. . . . [The pastor] must, therefore, stand before his people as one of them, a fellow-sinner, and yet in the full dignity and authority of his office, which he "strives to adorn with a holy life and conversation." . . . He stands before the congregation as the bearer of the office of Word and Sacrament upon which the congregation is dependent.[4]

This leads to another question which the Lutheran churches (and others too) ought to face squarely. It is all very well to insist that preaching and the administration of the sacraments are the sole functions of the ministry of the Word; but anyone who knows anything about the life and work of the churches today is aware that these are not the sole functions of the ordained ministry. The contemporary minister, in addition to preaching the Word and administering the sacraments, must fulfil so many other functions that these obligations frequently tend to overshadow those purposes for which he was ordained. Giving due regard to this fact, H. Richard Niebuhr has seriously proposed

Minutes, 1952, pp. 553-54.

that an appropriate title for the contemporary minister would be "pastoral director." [5] He points out that "the place in which the minister mainly functions always signalizes the Church's idea of his task." When the minister is primarily the priest that place is the altar; when he is primarily the preacher that place is the pulpit; when he is primarily the teacher that place is the parish education building. Today that place is the (central) office "from which he directs the activities of the church." The temptation of the contemporary minister is to become a "big operator," and to regard a dictating machine and a competent secretary as of more importance than vestments and a competent acolyte!

Distressed by this development, many ministers and churches have sought to correct the situation by adding to the staffs of congregations administrative assistants, directors of Christian education, directors of music, youth directors, parish workers, consulting psychologists, group work experts, etc. This trend is in many respects commendable, but our polity has not caught up with our practice. In the first place, pastors are frequently called to staff positions in which they have little or no opportunity to fulfil "the sole functions" for which they were ordained. Secondly, unordained personnel who may carry almost the same responsibilities as the ordained "pseudo-pastors" on the staff are not given the status in the church which they deserve. This anomalous situation exists, of course, not only on the congregational level but also in specialized ministries of the church. In the field of college and university work, for example, church policy usually prohibits a full-time campus pastor from preaching the Word and administering the sacraments to *his* congregation, namely, the students committed to his care by the church. On the other hand, when students are committed to the care of a woman counselor, who exercises almost the same functions as many campus pastors, the church gives her no more status

---

[5] *The Purpose of the Church and Its Ministry* (New York: Harper, 1956), pp. 79ff.

(even though she may have a degree from a theological seminary) than the caretaker of the student center!

And so we come to the question hinted at a few minutes ago: *Has the time not arrived when the church ought to return to the New Testament concept of the ministry as being inclusive of many types of services, and establish offices other than that of Word and sacrament?* This is indeed a recommendation of the U.L.C.A. Commission on the Doctrine of the Ministry: "The church should, therefore, also give serious consideration to the setting up of other offices within the church." [6] What about an office of teaching? Or perhaps even an office of church administration? Such a step may not only eliminate much of the current ambivalence in the office of Word and sacrament, but may well revitalize the whole ministry of the church.

The role of the professional

When the ministry of the church is understood in a broad sense as inclusive of many types of services, questions of category and status immediately arise. Which of these services can be provided on a volunteer, part-time basis? Which services should be placed on a full-time remunerative basis? Of those services placed on a full-time remunerative basis, which should be regarded as professional? What is the role of the professional? Let us tackle the last question.

For the purpose at hand a professional is defined as a member of the household of faith who by virtue of his unique spiritual gifts and his specialized education or training provides skilled service in a given area on a remunerative basis. The service he gives is his occupation or a part of his occupation, the source or a source of his livelihood, his "bread and butter." The category of professionals includes such persons as pastors, directors of music or of Christian education or of youth activities, counselors

[6] *Minutes, 1952,* p. 555.

to students, chaplains, and so forth. They consider their service in the church as their "lifework."

The church exists to be the body of Christ and to witness to Christ everywhere. Within the life and mission of the church the professionals have a role to play and the laymen have a role to play, and it is important that these roles be distinguished and clarified.

As we have already noted, within the life of the church all Christians have a ministry to bring to each other, a mutual ministry to physical and spiritual needs in the household of faith. For the sake of good order as well as of increased effectiveness, however, the members of the household of faith appoint individuals to perform certain services on their behalf. Thus pastors are appointed to a ministry of Word and sacrament, parish workers are appointed to a ministry of visitation, and church school directors are appointed to one of education. Pastor, parish worker, and church school director are delegated certain responsibilities which they can perform well because they have the competence and the time to give to "building up the body of Christ." In fact, it can be said that in the task of "building up the body of Christ" those specially appointed, the professionals, carry the major responsibility.

The reverse is true with regard to the church's task of evangelism and service in the world. Here the major responsibility must be borne directly by the laity of the church. Witness must be indigenous if it is to be of maximum effectiveness. *Christ can best be made known in all walks of life by those who are identified with these walks of life.* If the gospel is to penetrate the labor unions it must be carried there by Christians who are bona fide and active members of the union. If the gospel is to penetrate the managerial level of industry it must be carried there by Christians who have status on that level. If the gospel is to penetrate the university it must be carried there by Christians who as students, teachers, administrators are natives of the academic community. If the gospel is to penetrate the inner chambers of government it must be carried there by Christians who command respect as members of the Senate, the State Department, or the White House staff. In relation to these highly important segments of contemporary life ecclesiastical professionals are outsiders; they don't belong. The only way that the church can fulfil her mission in relation to labor, to industrial management, to higher education, to government, and to other aspects of culture is through laymen and women who are insiders, who do belong!

What, then, is the role of the professionals with regard to the church's task of evangelism and service in the world? *The role of the professionals is to prepare and support the laity as they discharge their direct responsibility to witness in the secular world.* The effectiveness of lay witness and service depends to a very great degree upon how well this professional role is played. When it comes to evangelism the professionals are not on the front lines; they are behind the lines giving themselves to "the equipment of the saints" before they go into battle and to "the refreshment of the saints" as they return from the fray confused and exhausted.

And how do the professionals carry out their role of equipping and refreshing the saints? They do so by providing a ministry of Word and sacrament, a ministry of pastoral care, a ministry of teaching, a ministry of training in "strategy and tactics."

With reference to the mission of the church in the world, ordained clergymen have usually conceived their role to be that of exhortation and direct action. On the one hand, they have exhorted laymen from the pulpit to be Christian in their daily life and work, and they have frequently done this in ways which do not get at the basic issues which confront laymen in the secular world. And when occasionally the basic issues are identified, little or no guidance is offered as to how the layman can come to grips with the issues in relation to the Christian faith.

So often the consciences of the laity have been disturbed without any constructive action taking place on the front lines. On the other hand, so often the clergymen, noting the weakness of lay witness in the world and having a high regard for their own competence, have themselves attempted to penetrate the secular orders. Neither pulpit exhortation alone nor direct clerical action will yield significant gains in the workaday world for the gospel of Christ.

What is needed is a new understanding of the roles of the laity and of the professionals in the mission of the church. The laity have frequently been "inspired" but not equipped for battle; and the professionals have frequently dissipated their energies in frustrating forays into the secular world when they should have been preparing the laity for conquests on terrain the laity already know well. The proper role of the laity in a congregation is not to assist the pastor; the proper role of the pastor is to assist the laity to be the church militant. When laymen and laywomen assemble at the church facilities during the week it should not be for the purpose of being preached at yet again or of being entertained, but for the purpose of undergoing serious training as witnesses of Christ and of realistically devising strategies for consolidating victories won or for establishing new beachheads on behalf of the church in our communities and in our culture.[7]

Recruitment for professional service

Pastors and laymen are keenly aware of the current shortage

[7] For an elaboration of the point of view expressed in this section the reader is referred to the report of Section VI of the Evanston Assembly of the World Council of Churches on "The Laity—the Christian in His Vocation" (*Evanston Speaks* pp. 59-67, published by the World Council of Churches), and an article by Hans-Ruedi Weber entitled "The Ministry of the Laity in the Missionary Outreach of the Church" in *The Student World*, XLIX, No. 3, 221-36 (published by the World Student Christian Federation).

of qualified personnel for professional service in the church. The cry of alarm has been sounded by interdenominational agencies and denominational headquarters. The National Council of the Churches of Christ in the U.S.A. reports that the Protestant church bodies need twenty-five thousand pastors to fill fifteen thousand vacant parishes and ten thousand new positions, while only sixty-eight hundred students graduated in 1956 from all Protestant seminaries. In the United Lutheran Church in America the 1957 shortage of pastors reached 439, and the Board of Higher Education has estimated an accumulating annual shortage of two hundred in the foreseeable future. There were only 191 graduates from U.L.C.A. seminaries in 1957 to fill 439 vacancies. The United Lutheran Church in America needs now 60 per cent more seminary graduates, but the number of pretheological students presently enrolled in colleges and universities will barely maintain the status quo. A comparable shortage also exists with regard to unordained church staff personnel, such as directors of Christian education, parish workers, counselors to students in universities, youth directors, and social workers in church institutions.

Many reasons have been advanced to explain the shortage of personnel for church staff positions. A few of them were cited in the first lecture. For one thing, the number of church members and congregations has been growing at an accelerated rate since World War II and it is estimated that the acceleration will continue. Not only are there heavy demands for pastors for new congregations, but as established congregations increase in size to three, four, five, and six thousand members greatly enlarged staffs become necessary. And this phenomenal increase in members and in congregations has, in turn, required more and more staff members in the general work of the churches.

A second reason for the shortage is the trend in retirement and longevity of pastors. Time was when most pastors remained at their positions until death because, financially speaking, they had no alternative. With the inauguration of sound pension plans by the churches and with the opening of social security benefits to the clergy the retirement of pastors at the age of 65 is becoming more or less routine. Thus, the annual loss of pastors through retirement is increasing rapidly. There is also evidence that the loss of pastors by death before retirement is steadily increasing, doubtless reflecting the mounting pressures under which the ministry is carried on today.

In the third place, the "natural man" inducements to enter secular occupations have become extremely appealing. Put negatively, a minister no longer plays a major role in American culture or in the life of the typical American community just because he is a minister. "Benefit of clergy" has almost become an anachronism. Put positively, the opportunities of realizing the current American dream of a home of your own with wall-to-wall carpeting in every room and with two cars in the garage; of an income sufficiently large to furnish a home comfortably, to send the children to the best schools, to enjoy a full social life, and to retire early; and of sufficient leisure time to engage in extensive hobbies, to maintain an edge over your neighbor in regard to books, the theatre, and the arts, and to enjoy extended vacations—the opportunities of realizing this dream are far greater in almost any other field than in the ministry.

A fourth factor is the reverse of the third: professional service in American church bodies no longer demands the heroic sacrifices which used to challenge hardy souls and those made of the stuff of martyrs. For such spirits professional service in the church has become too secularized. Although the possibility of a minister realizing the great American dream is remote, the clergy by and large live comfortably with a considerable degree of security. Even missionaries are transported to and from their fields of labor in stratocruisers, are furnished with station wagons and tape-recorders, and live in houses equipped with automatic appliances!

The list could be greatly extended, but a fifth cause of the personnel crisis in the churches deserves mention if not emphasis, namely, the secularization of the concept of vocation, of calling. From the time when "to be called" meant something very special and very significant we have arrived at a time when vocation is merely a synonym for occupation, vocational guidance is a pseudo-science largely in the control of naturalists, who regard professional service in the church as a third-rate occupation with a decidedly limited appeal.

So much for the diagnosis! What about a prescription? In a sense these lectures as a whole are offered as a contribution to the healing of the malaise which has befallen vocation. Certain specific comments are in order, however, regarding recruitment for professional service in the church.

1. *A fresh and invigorating sense of Christian vocation, of God's calling in Christ, must appear in the household of faith and lay claim to the total life of every member of the household.*

If such a sense now existed in the household of faith there would be candidates aplenty for professional service in the church. That is to say, if the members of the household were really open to the call of God, he would take care of the personnel needs of his church. To borrow a phrase from Gerhard Tersteegen's hymn, "God is calling yet"—the problem is that we do not hear. This is not pietism; this is realism, or else our faith is but fancy and vocation is a fraud.

Recruitment techniques are frequently emergency measures to deal with a situation which should not exist anyhow! In other words, recruitment plans often deal with symptoms rather than with the disease itself. There can be no permanent solution to the personnel crisis of the churches short of a renewal of the life and mission of the household of faith. This is not to rule out a program of recruitment, rightly conceived, but it is to insist that the root problem is one of motivation which will be solved only in the realm of the spirit.

2. *The nature and significance of professional service in the church must receive clarification if effective recruitment is to be done.*

Some of the ambiguities and inadequacies of the current policy and practice of the churches regarding such professional service have already been discussed in this lecture, and certain suggestions have been offered. Underlying these suggestions is the conviction that the Lutheran understanding of the ministry needs to be broadened so that offices other than that of Word and sacrament can be established.

Scores of pastors are now holding church positions with job analyses which do not require the preaching of the Word and the administration of the sacraments. Either a new office ought to be established which is more appropriate to the responsibilities entailed or these positions should be filled by laymen. The more extensive employment of competent laymen will cost the churches more money, but the additional investment will yield at least two valuable dividends, namely, the release of much-needed pastors for bona fide ministries of Word and sacrament and progress toward recovery of the integrity of the office of Word and sacrament itself.

Another place where clarification is long overdue is the role of women in professional service in the church. In the Lutheran churches the diaconate has been a fully recognized and respected channel through which women who wish to make a total life commitment to the church can serve. Next to the deaconess in status has been the woman missionary. Outside the diaconate and the mission field the contributions of women through other types of professional church service have been extensive and magnificent. Nevertheless, church bodies have persistently discriminated against the women they have employed! Even when women in church staff positions equal pastors in native ability, training, education, and experience the pastors usually receive preferential treatment in terms of tenure, income, housing provisions, and retirement arrangements. It is to be expected that professional service in the church should involve a certain degree of renunciation of the good things of life, but why should the church expect greater "sacrifice" from its women employees than from its pastors?

3. *The church must be more precise and consistent in its definition of a call to professional service in the church, especially as seen in relation to service in the secular world.*

A great deal of mystery is still associated with a call to the ministry. This mystery can even excite the interest of the editors of such a secular magazine as *The New Yorker* to the point of their publishing an article entitled "The Presbyterian Call System." [8] The author, a descendant of several generations of clergymen, never "got the call." From observing his many relatives who did get the call, however, he arrived at these conclusions:

They could receive the call almost anytime, but they usually got it, if they were going to get it at all, about the time they finished preparatory school and were ready to go to college. . . . Men could get the call any place, but it always happened to them when they were alone. . . . When they got it, they knew what it was. . . . The call entailed a direct communication between the recipient and God. . . . Nobody knew much about the precise nature of the procedure except God and the men who had themselves received the call. . . . In giving them the call, God evidently exacted a promise of secrecy, for some reason known only to God.

This description of the call to the ministry should not be lightly dismissed as a journalistic caricature; it is the view held by the vast majority of people both inside and outside the church, and the church has not taken seriously enough its obligation to correct such a view.

The Protestant churches have, of course, been in general agreement that the call to the ordained ministry involves four ele-

[8] May 18, 1957.

ments: the call into the church, the secret or inner call, the providential call, and the ecclesiastical call.[9] Except for the fourth element, which establishes the locus of service, is the call to the ordained ministry essentially different from the calling of a physician, a teacher, or an architect? To this question the churches have given a confused and confusing answer. To reiterate: a great deal of "straight talking" must be done to dispel the clouds which now envelop the portals into professional service in the church.

4. *The church must maintain a comprehensive program of recruitment which emphasizes needs and qualifications, and which is related to the counseling services of the schools.*

It must be comprehensive in that it should begin at the primary age and continue through the elementary and secondary levels into the college and university years. Until recently the two extremes of this span of experience have received little attention. The most promising recent developments have taken place in the private and public institutions of higher learning, with reference to which H. Richard Niebuhr reports as follows:

No radical changes have taken place during the last twenty or thirty years in the recruitment practices of the (church) schools and the denominations. Insofar as increased enrollments (in the seminaries) are due to recruitment programs it is the intensification and organization of such programs in several denominations that may be held accountable. The extension of recruitment activity into state and municipal universities together with the development of student Christian work on such campuses may be the most significant change that has occurred. One denomination reports that it can trace the increases in its theological student body almost wholly to these sources; it is receiving as many applications for admission to seminaries from denominational colleges as it has in the past, but not many more; it has doubled its theological enrollment because of the influx of students from schools not church related.[10]

[9] Cf. H. Richard Niebuhr, *op. cit.*, p. 64.
[10] Niebuhr, Williams, and Gustafson, *The Advancement of Theological Education* (New York: Harper, 1957), pp. 13-14.

A recruitment program should emphasize (a) the personnel needs of the church and (b) the qualifications which must be met for entrance into professional church service. Motivation ought not to be a major emphasis of a recruitment program for two reasons. For one thing, as noted above, motivation for professional church service should be a normal by-product of the renewal of the life and mission of the church through Word and sacrament. For another thing, when motivation is stressed in a recruitment program it frequently takes on the character of high-pressure campaigning, the benefits of which are extremely dubious. A recruitment program should present the facts (regarding needs and qualifications) as attractively and as dramatically as possible through publications, films, conferences, personal interviews, exploratory experiences, testing, tours, etc. A person who is responding to God's summons to service can then respond in terms of the facts, thus maintaining a maximum degree of objectivity at the point of decision-making.

The church must recognize that the schools are today playing the major role in occupational counseling. Hundreds of high schools have full-time career counselors, and thousands of schools have rather extensive testing programs. It is essential, therefore, that the churches maintain good relationships with guidance personnel in community schools as well as with guidance associations. One of the most encouraging signs on the horizon is the possibility of increasing co-ordination between the career counseling of the schools and the deep concerns of the church for the wise investment of life and talents.

A great deal more could be said about recruitment for professional service in the church. The Protestant denominations are developing increasingly effective recruitment programs. Within the Lutheran church bodies a major effort ought to be made to integrate, at least to some degree, the multifarious recruitment activities now under way or being planned.

It must be remembered, however, that the key to effective

recruitment is not so much programs as persons. Whether or not Johnny gives serious consideration to service in the church as his lifework will depend in large measure upon the kind of persons with whom he is closely associated. A survey of almost two thousand theological and pretheological students enrolled in fifty-seven educational institutions representing twenty denominations indicated that the persons who first turned their attention to the ministry were as follows: pastors, 34 per cent; parents, 28.6 per cent; church leaders other than pastors, 15.7 per cent; teachers, 8.9 per cent; friends, 8.9 per cent; wives, 3.9 per cent. How important it is that those engaged professionally in the work of the church "walk worthily of the calling to which [they] have been called." And how significant it is that, numerically speaking, lay persons exercised greater influence than the clergy.[11]

And so we come to the end of our consideration not only of professional service in the church but also of Christian vocation in all its meanings and manifestations. It has been the theme of these lectures that Christian vocation makes the difference between mere existence and life transformed by the purpose and power of God. Such is the life of Everyman whom the Holy Spirit calls by the gospel, enlightens with his gifts, and sanctifies and keeps in the true faith; even as he calls, gathers, enlightens, and sanctifies the whole church of Christ.

God calls his children to be with him and to be with each other in his household, the fellowship of the forgiven and the forgiving. This fellowship is known supremely in the breaking of bread together at the family meal, in the Sacrament of the Lord's Supper. And God calls his children to service in all their relationships. After the family meal there are errands to be run; the doing of tasks is the sequel to breaking bread together. For God's call gives his children both life and mission. That this gift may be ours should be our constant prayer.

---

[11] This survey as reported in *The Lutheran Companion* (Nov. 13, 1957) was made by Prof. Ralph A. Felton of Drew Theological Seminary.

SELECTED BIBLIOGRAPHY

Readers are referred to the excellent "Bibliography on Work and Vocation" prepared by Robert S. Michaelsen for the volume entitled *Work and Vocation*, ed. by John Oliver Nelson (New York: Harper & Bros., 1954). This bibliography, which lists more than two hundred items, is conveniently arranged into sections on the basis of the character and content of the publications. Neither space nor good sense justifies the duplication here of such a catalogue of resource material. Consequently, only those items of some importance which have appeared since 1954 or which for other reasons are not included in the Michaelsen bibliography are listed below by way of a supplement.

BALY, DENIS. *Chosen Peoples.* Philadelphia: Christian Education Pr., 1956. (An interpretation of the concept of corporate vocation with reference not only to the church but also to the nation and to the university.)

BERGSTRAND, WILTON E., Marjorie Axelton, Carl L. Manfred. *Adventuring with Christ in the Church Staff Vocations.* Minneapolis: Augustana Lutheran Church, 1956.

BONHOEFFER, DIETRICH. *The Cost of Discipleship.* Translated by R. H. Fuller. New York: Macmillan Co., 1948. (A moving interpretation of calling as self-renouncing commitment.)

DEMILLE, CANON G. E. (ed.). *Man at Work in God's World.* New York: Longmans, Green & Co., 1956. (Papers delivered at the Church and Work Congress sponsored by the Episcopal Church in Albany, October 19-20, 1955.)

FORELL, GEORGE W. *Faith Active in Love.* New York: American Pr., 1954. (Cf. pp. 120ff. for an illuminating discussion of Luther's view of vocation in relation to the "orders.")

———. "Work and the Christian Calling," *The Lutheran Quarterly*, VIII, No. 2 (May 1956).

HALL, CAMERON P. (ed.) *You, Your Church, and Your Job.* New York: N.C.C.C.U.S.A., 1955. (A study and discussion booklet on the report of Section VI, "The Laity—the Christian in His Vocation," of the 1954 Assembly of the World Council of Churches.)

HAZELTON, ROGER. *God's Way with Man.* New York: Abingdon Pr., 1956. (A fresh examination of the doctrine of providence in relation to contemporary thought and to the concept of vocation. Cf. especially chap. 7, "Technics and Vocation.")

HEINECKEN, MARTIN J. "Luther and the 'Orders of Creation' in Relation to a Doctrine of Work and Vocation," *The Lutheran Quarterly,* IV, No. 4 (November 1952).

KANE, GEORGE L. (ed.). *Lay Workers for Christ.* Westminster: Newman Pr., 1957. (A product of the lay apostolate movement in the Roman church: autobiographical sketches of Roman Catholics who have found a "vocation" as laymen.)

"Laborers into His Harvest," a special number of *The International Journal of Religious Education,* XXX, No. 5 (January 1957).

"The Laity: The Christian in His Vocation," in W. A. VISSER 'T HOOFT (ed.), *The Evanston Report* (The Second Assembly of the World Council of Churches, 1954), Sec. VI. New York: Harper & Bros., 1955.

"The Laity," a special number of *The Student World,* XLIX, No. 3.

"The Lay Apostolate in the Roman Catholic Church," a special number of *Laity,* No. I (February 1956). Bulletin of the Department of the Laity, World Council of Churches.

LETTS, HAROLD C. (ed.). *Christian Social Responsibility.* A Symposium in Three Volumes. Vol. I, *Existence Today;* Vol. II, *The Lutheran Heritage;* Vol. III, *Life in Community.* Philadelphia: Muhlenberg Pr., 1957. (Cf. indexes on "Vocation.")

LUTHER, MARTIN. *Luther's Works,* American Ed., Vols. 12, 13, 21, 22, 31, 32, 40. St. Louis: Concordia, 1956—; and Philadelphia: Muhlenberg Pr., 1957—

———. *The Works of Martin Luther,* Philadelphia Ed. 6 vols. Philadelphia: Muhlenberg Pr., 1915-1945.

———. *The Precious and Sacred Writings of Martin Luther,* ed. J. N. LENKER. Minneapolis: Lutherans of All Lands Co., 1905. (Attention is directed to Vol. X, *Church Postils for Advent, Christmas, and Epiphany Sermons*, which is the only English translation of this important material for an understanding of Luther's concept of vocation.)

————. *The Table Talk of Martin Luther*, ed. Thomas S. Kepler. New York: World Pub. Co., 1952.

MATTSON, KARL E. *The Glory of Common Tasks*. Chicago: National Lutheran Council, 1952.

MILLER, ALEXANDER. *The Renewal of Man*. Garden City, N. Y.: Doubleday & Co., 1955. (Cf. chap. 7, "The Calling of a Christian Man.")

NELSON, JOHN OLIVER. *A Listing of Church Vocations*. New York: N.C.C.C.U.S.A., n.d.

————. *Opportunities in Protestant Religious Vocations*. New York: Vocational Guidance Manuals, 1952.

———— (ed.). *Work and Vocation*. New York: Harper & Bros., 1954. (In the form of a symposium, this is perhaps the best single volume dealing with the concept of vocation in relation to the contemporary world.)

NIEBUHR, H. RICHARD. *The Purpose of the Church and Its Ministry*. (Part I of the report on "The Survey of Theological Education in the United States and Canada.") New York: Harper & Bros., 1956.

———— and DANIEL D. WILLIAMS (eds.). *The Ministry in Historical Perspective*. (Part II of the report on "The Survey of Theological Education in the United States and Canada.") New York: Harper & Bros., 1956.

————, ————, and JAMES M. GUSTAFSON. *The Advancement of Theological Education*. (Part III of the report on "The Survey of Theological Education in the United States and Canada.") New York: Harper & Bros., 1957.

Occupational Outlook Handbook. 1957 ed., Bulletin 1215. Published by the United States Department of Labor, Bureau of Labor Statistics. Washington: U. S. Government Printing Office, 1957. (Employment information on major occupations for use in guidance.)

PIPER, OTTO A. "The Meaning of Work," *Theology Today*, XIV, No. 2 (July 1957).

RICHARDSON, ALAN. *The Biblical Doctrine of Work.* London: S.C.M. Pr., 1952.

SAYERS, DOROTHY L. *Creed or Chaos?* New York: Harcourt, Brace and Co., 1949. (Cf. chap. VI, "Why Work?")

SOUTHARD, SAMUEL. *Counseling for Church Vocations.* Nashville: Broadman Pr., 1957.

STEERE, DOUGLAS V. *Work and Contemplation.* New York: Harper & Bros., 1957.

Steps to a Church Vocation. Published by the Board of Christian Education, Presbyterian Church in the U. S. A. (A manual of procedures "for the calling and care of candidates for the ministry and for commissioned church work.")

TORRANCE, T. F. *Royal Priesthood.* Edinburgh: Oliver and Boyd, 1955. (A stimulating biblical study of corporate vocation in relation to the doctrine of the church and the ministry.)

"The Training of the Laity for Their Ministry in the World," a special number of *Laity*, No. II (June 1956). Bulletin of The Department of the Laity, World Council of Churches.

TRUEBLOOD, ELTON. "Christian Faith and Daily Work," *The Christian Century*, LXXIII, No. 35 (August 29, 1956).

WHYTE, WILLIAM H., JR. *The Organization Man.* Garden City, N. Y.: Doubleday and Co., 1957. (Cf. chap. 2, "The Decline of the Protestant Ethic.")

WINGREN, GUSTAF. "The Christian's Calling According to Luther," *The Augustana Quarterly*, XXI (1942).

———. "The Church and the Calling," *The Augustana Quarterly*, XXVI, No. 4 (October 1947).

———. *Luther on Vocation.* Translated by Carl C. Rasmussen. Philadelphia: Muhlenberg Pr., 1957.

WIRT, SHERWOOD E. "Is Work So Holy?" *The Christian Century*, LXXIII, No. 35 (August 29, 1956).

The Worker Priests. Translated by John Petrie. London: Routledge and Kegan Paul, 1956. (A "collective documentation" of a much-heralded but finally condemned attempt to penetrate the industrial order with the gospel.)

Type used in this book
Body, 10 on 13 and 9 on 11 Janson
Display, Janson
Paper: R.R.R. Standard White Antique